Sound
the
Trumpet

The Call of God to His Church

By

Prophetess Margaret Ade Odusanya

Sound the Trumpet: The Call of God to His Church

ISBN: 978-1-909206-04-5

Published by Divine Grace Enterprises Limited.

DIVINE GRACE
ENTERPRISE LIMITED.
"For with Grace Enterprise, nothing shall be impossible"

Cover Design by: Zoe Communications Limited.
Scripture quotations are from the King James Version of the Bible.
Printed in the United Kingdom and the United States of America.

CONTENTS

ᘓᙠᘓᙠ

DEDICATION

ᘓᘔᘓᘔ

I dedicate this book to Almighty God the Father, God the Son—Jesus Christ, my Saviour and God the Holy Spirit—who leads and guides my life. You are the giver of this assignment and these visions. You are the one who healed my broken heart and poured the oil of your healing grace upon my life.

I dedicate this book to all the saints of God who hunger to please and to walk with Him closely and intimately. This book is also dedicated to my fellow labourers in the vineyard of God. May He bless you all as you walk in the path of the perfect will of the Lord, in Jesus' name. Amen.

ACKNOWLEDGMENTS

ങ്ങരു

I would like to thank my precious Holy Spirit who brought me this mission in the month of May 2011, during my ninety days on the mountain. Then, after six weeks of preparing for the Lord's hand to guide my pen, the Holy Spirit came to me and said, "Get up and get started on the book." I fretted and said, "Lord, I don't know what to write yet." But He said, "Go, and I will empower you." Today, I give glory to the Lord for this book, completed in His name and for His glory.

I would like to thank my father in the Lord, Dr. D.K. Olukoya, the General Overseer of Mountain of Fire and Miracles Ministries Worldwide, for his fatherly love and for believing in the call of God upon my life and for always empowering me. You are the angel that God used to bring me out of the world and into the kingdom of God. Heaven will reward you a million times and your anointing will never run dry, in Jesus' name. Amen.

In the chapter on the Holy Spirit, some of the information is taken from Dr. Olukoya's pamphlet entitled: Deliverance Through the Watches, for which work and whose kind permission to quote herein I am eternally grateful.

My special thanks goes to one of the great women generals of our time, Rev. Mrs Yinka Badejo, the President of Dew of Heaven Ministry in Lagos, Nigeria for writing the foreword to this book. May God richly bless you ma, in Jesus' name. Amen.

I would also like to thank Reverend Margie Grotto Fleurant, who has been a blessing to me since my time in (Faith International Training School), a Bible college in Fort Myers, Florida, U.S.A. Her expertise and experience helped shape the final form of this book. By endorsing it she has offered me practical and spiritual support. Thank you for your blessings and love. You are a breath of fresh air to me, and the ministries. God of heaven will rain His blessings upon your life and works, in Jesus' name. Amen.

In addition I would like to offer thanks to: Pastor Wale Babatunde of World Harvest Church, London—whose book: Britain Has Fallen gave me a great insights. Some quotations from that book are used in chapter six: "Wake-Up, Sleeping Churches".

Dr Earl D. Johnson, my mentor in California, who has also been like a father to me. Pa, God bless you and all that you have done for me to encourage me in the work of the Lord. I would also like to thank Rev. Gene Ojegba, my prayer partner and friend as well as my childhood friend, Pastor Honeybell Silas. Thank you both for your support, for always being there for me and for the true and abiding friendships you have shown me. God bless you both.

Finally, I would like to thank my husband, Pastor JK Odusanya, for his encouragement and support— my children Chibuezeh, Adanma and Ugochi, my elder brother, Prophet Michael Mayaki, and my sisters— for all your support and prayers. Without all of you my ministerial assignment would have been a much harder, lonelier undertaking. Thank you all so very much.

FOREWORD

CRURCRUR

I n The Acts of the Apostles, to paraphrase some of the things Luke said...all that Jesus began to do and to teach until the day He was taken up, after He had given commands through the Holy Spirit to the apostles whom He had chosen (Acts 1:2). Evidently, our Lord and Saviour Jesus Christ only then began to teach and to do! The narration in that very important book of the Bible also showed that the Lord continued 'to do and to teach' after His ascension in the Book of Acts by the Holy Spirit. I wish to boldly state that the Lord had never once stopped doing and teaching even though the Book of Acts ended in its twenty-eighth chapter.

The Book of Acts is not yet closed. All through the history of the church, the Lord has been doing great deeds and teaching His people. When you review the life and ministry of such vessels of the Lord as the author, you will agree that the record of the Lord's 'doings' is still going on!

The Book of Acts among other things reflects the dealings of the Holy Spirit with some of the Lord's chosen vessels. Reading between the lines of this book you will unmistakably see the dealings of the Lord with the author of this book which makes for very exciting and racy reading—

similar feelings that you might have experienced reading the Book of Acts. The reason is not far fetched. The author's experiences that are chronicled in this book were undoubtedly produced by the same unction that operated in and among the apostles and disciples of the early church, as captured in The Acts of the Apostles!

The author sets out this book in ten chapters. It opens with the gracious dealings of a loving Lord with a precious daughter whom He revealed Himself to through her many tribulations. He won her heart when His atoning and sacrificial death on the cross became personally meaningful. The Lord doted on her, cleaning up her heart from the effects of demonic abuse— which left such deep spiritual wounds that only the Great Physician and Baptiser with the Holy Spirit can deal with. He emptied her of the filth of that past life—filled, decorated and garnished her life with the treasure of His mighty presence and His gifts. Again, the Lord has demonstrated through His dealings with the author that He seeks out each person who is yielded to Him so as to reach out to many others who are yet to know Him.

This book, in chronicling some of the Lord's dealings with Prophetess Margaret confirms that the Lord bestows both grace and gifts to such yielded persons, utilizing every real life experience both good and bad—to attain His highest purposes not only in the subject, but even more so, in the lives of those who will come in contact with the subject. The travails of Paul the apostle are essentially the thrust of the next three chapters (two-four). Chapter five illustrates the fact that the Lord seeks to have a deeper intimacy with the one He chooses to use in any meaningful way. In this respect, no child of God can do without the marvellous gift of hearing the voice of the Holy Spirit. As the Lord moves with and through His servant, this ability, as shown in the many life experiences of the author becomes very invaluable. The same thread runs through the following two chapters (six and seven).

The closing three chapters deal with the prophetic and the strategic ministry to the Body as this age draws to a close. This seeks to lead and guide the Body (especially the leadership) as the church wrestles with damaging and distracting antics of the adversary. The Lord, it seems would not leave the church without a witness with a telescope, as it were, into the end of the age. This I believe, the author wants the church to know how vital it is for every believer to walk closely with the Master so as to please Him to the end.

It is on this high note that the author makes most of the title of this must-read book Sound the Trumpets: The Call of God to His Church. I recommend this book to every serious Christian, leader and follower alike. If your goal is to serve the Lord that you love, please read it! If your goal is to make heaven after a fruitful service here on earth, please read this book. If you are yearning to hear the Master's voice saying: "Well done..." Please do not miss out from reading this book. I pray that the Holy Spirit's fire will burn through you afresh as you read and may your life never be the same after grasping the author's impassioned messages.

Shalom!
Rev. Mrs. A. A. Badejo
Dew of Heaven Ministry

ENDORSEMENTS

ᏩᏐᏆᏐ

M argaret was formally a student of mine at Faith International Training School, Fort Myers, Florida. From the moment I saw her, the anointing and calling on her life was evident. She is a woman of the Word of God and carries a strong prophetic calling to reach the nations. In Sound the Trumpet: A Call of God to His Church you will hear Margaret's voice and her words will be a catalyst for change in your life and ministry.

Rev. Margie Grotto Fleurant
President of Rivers Ministries
New Jersey, U.S.A.

Prophetess Margaret is one of God's rare, seasoned, tried and proven servants. I have known her for a long while now, and have grown to love her as a sister and ministerial colleague from the womb of the Spirit. She is my prayer partner and very passionate about the LORD, a quality I admire so much in her. Her love for God is genuine. I have always known Margaret to be a tenacious God seeker—with prayer and in fasting.

See her passion in the chapter five where she writes

about her "Precious Holy Spirit." We very much complement each other as she is highly gifted in hearing God speaking into her ears, while He shows me the pictures of things, as we pray together. Also we are both called by God to gather women for the purpose of intercession.

This book is truly from the womb of the Holy Spirit and I know, once you start reading it, you will never want to drop it, until you have read from cover to cover. I employ you to open up your heart as you read, and you will surely be blessed.

Reverend Gene Ojegba
President of True Vine
International Ministries,
London

The author of this beautiful piece is a very gifted child of God especially in the area of the prophetic. She has an outstanding understanding of prophetic ministry and this work is an attempt to communicate it with such deep insight for the benefit and blessing of the reader. What you are holding in your hand is a book that can transform your life. The author's experiences chronicled in this book were undoubtedly produced by the same unction that operated in and among the apostles and disciples of the early church as captured in the Book of Acts.

Sound the Trumpets is an encounter with the Trinity. It is a personal journey in the school of life expressing the agape love of God in redeeming the lost no matter how hopeless her case became (I Timothy 1:12-15). God redefines her life. God is also on the look out for a yielded vessel that He can empower for His noble use and purpose. He craves for deeper intimacy with the redeemed. You need to hear the voice of the Holy Spirit through the author's many life experiences. Prophetess Margaret shares the truth of the prophetic unction and its strategic ministry to the body of Christ. God will always have a witness in every age and dispensation therefore there is always a need for the redeemed to maintain a close walk with the Master to the end.

I strongly recommend this book for every believer, Christian bookshop and library as it makes a very exciting and racy reading, similar feelings that you would have experienced reading the Book of Acts.

Rev. Yinka Badejo
Dew of Heaven Ministry

INTRODUCTION

ෆ૪ා૯૪ා

I give glory to the Father, to the Son, Jesus Christ, and the most Precious Holy Spirit. This book is meant for those in the vineyard of God who truly want to serve the Lord faithfully with all their heart and soul. It is meant to aid us in reflecting upon and examining our work as ministers and as believers. When we embrace the truth of God's word and faithfully do all that He has commanded us to do, then, there will be rewards for us here on earth and in heaven. Let us open our hearts and hear what God has in store for us.

Sound the Trumpet!
The Call of God to His Church!

Sound the Trumpet The Call of God to His Church

1

Recognising the Gifts and Talents within Our Churches
CX80CX80

Many people's spiritual gifts die with them as a result of the inability of pastors and ministers to recognise such fortunate blessings amongst their members.

A number of years ago I belonged to such a church—a church that lacked the ability to discern my own spiritual gifts, a church that could not recognise the call of God and His influence upon my life. Consequently, the calling of God was neglected and the true core of my being suffered as a result—although God's hand was upon me then, and always be— forever. Often before events happened within that church, God revealed to me what was forthcoming. I used to tell some of the elders what the Lord had told me. A few nicknamed me 'Joseph the dreamer', in denial of the truth, not realising that the gift of prophecy was working through me.

The Bible says that the "steps of the righteous are ordered by the Lord". God knows our destinies and the assignments He has given each and every one of His children. When God's hand is upon you, He will redirect your steps in order to make you a more perfect instrument of His will. In my case, that began when He redirected my steps to another ministry (Mountain of Fire and Miracles Ministries) under the Leadership of Dr D.K. Olukoya, in 2004.

I thank God that He did, because Dr D.K. Olukoya was the vessel God used to detect the gift and the calling that would shape my life. An absence or lack of good mentors or leaders— leaders who can discern their flock's individual callings and help them on their paths, leads to many people not achieving their God-given destinies.

During the course of my work in the house of God, I have met many people whom I can discern—who are meant to be great leaders of the future, yet who are still unaware of their purpose and who are doing nothing in the house of God to discover it. It is sad, indeed, that so much potential and so many destinies are wasted in the lives of people whom God is calling to engage in great works for His glory and in His name. They come to church not knowing their true callings.

Many a time when I have been ministering at a church, God— by His grace— will show me the lives and destinies of many in the congregation who have not realised their God-given potentials. God has placed us, His ministers, into the lives of our members to act as shepherds, to help guide them their God-given assignments and callings. It is our role to recognise the gifts within our members early on, in order to direct them to the rightful area of their individual calling. May the eyes of our understanding be opened so that we can see and sense the gifts that God has given to those within our congregations.

Whilst some leaders are aware of the individuals who have gifts within their ministries but sadly out of selfishness and fear that those 'stars' will shine above them, they dismiss and subdue those so honoured by the Holy Spirit. If you are among those whose gifts and callings have been subdued—as you read this book, the God of heaven will redirect your footsteps in Jesus' name. Amen.

✕❧✦❀✦❧✦✕
Working from Our Churches

Smaller groups within the main body of the church have the benefit of being able to identify individuals who have God-given talents and determine the ways and in which areas they have been blessed and gifted. These groups can work more rapidly in bringing these gifts and abilities to the fore.

In the body of Christ, God has placed his gifts within us under five different areas of calling: apostles, prophets, pastors, evangelists and teachers. But the central purpose for each and all of these vocations is for the instruction and edification of the body of Christ. Ideally, a church should bear congregations and leaderships who are comprised of people directed onto all these God paths.

The role of pastors and elders in the church is to be able to recognise to which calling God is leading an individual. We never know if the next Billy Graham is among the people we are pastoring. We do not know if God is raising the next Dr Olukoya among our congregation. We—as leaders—will be held accountable, by God for talents and gifts within the body of Christ if they are wasted; if we do not seek out and nurture them intently. At the gates of heaven, pastors and ministers will be judged most harshly for our lapses and our lacking, because we are the ones to whom the laws of God have been entrusted. It truly saddens my heart to see how many talents and gifts are lost and unrecognised— their possessors never achieving or even knowing their divine destinies.

The youth, the Bible tells us, are our future. But what future can the youth have when they are unaware, when they are never even shown that there are such divinely blessed gifts and talents inside of them? The revival, the Lord has shown me, is going to start with the youth, but how can they become the agents of change they are destined to be if they don't even know that they possess these gifts?

In Malachi 2 verse 7: The Bible tells us that, "The words of a priest's lip should preserve knowledge of God, and people should go to him for instruction, for the priest is the messenger of the Lord of Heaven's Armies."

So we have seen it written that the lips of the priest are meant to bring instruction and preserve knowledge, but when we do not discover the gifts and talents in our church members, what instruction and knowledge are we going to preserve? These failings also sadden the Holy Spirit, for in the absence of proper teaching and understanding about God's gifts, He is not allowed to come forth in an individual's life— to make them ready for what God has called them to do.

Unfortunately, in several of the larger churches many are going simply so as to boast that they attend that particular institution. The true reasons for going to the church are neglected, often never fulfilled. God is aggrieved with those leaders who are too busy to tend to their flocks (whether with speaking engagements or with the church business) rather than the business of the home church. Tragically they are too busy with so many church programmes that do not glorify the Lord, agendas and plans that exclude the true mandate and heart of the Lord and his work.

The Lord, working through me, and those who have shaped the message of this book is sounding an alarm bell, an instruction to us all to mend our ways and to begin again to sincerely nurture our flocks, help them discover the divine direction intended for them. The Bible tells us that many are called, but few are chosen. How then can the people know that they have been called if they do not know that they have been chosen for the work of the ministry when they are subdued, when their divinely- granted potentials are not realised?

The Holy Spirit is grieved by the way in which some shepherds are treating their flocks—flocks that they have abandoned to the wolves. Those who are hurting and needing care are forgotten. Those who are sick and unattended, those whose lives are scattered are ignored. Who is caring for them? Who is reaching out to them in love? Of course some shepherds are doing good work in the name of the Lord, and He wishes to commend us for our efforts and promise that heaven will reward us sincerely for our good work and commitment. For those of us who are yet to get to that of mark of perfection, God is using this book to speak into our hearts.

As a prophet of God, there are times the assignment might be a tough one, as this has been, but I have no choice in the matter. What the Lord speaks to me in (the) secret place: my role is to bring his Word into the open for all to hear and for all to share in what God the Almighty requires of us.

God is counting on us, the shepherds of the Lord. The Holy Spirit will empower us to fulfil our mandates as servants of the living God; we are called to serve and not to be served—as others, sadly, are doing. Our perfect example is Jesus Himself, who humbled himself to wash the feet of the disciples.

What Steps Are Needed to Ensure These Gifts Are Not Wasted?

Sunday School teachers, who are given the opportunity to carefully observe the children in their care, must also have the ability to see and understand the inborn blessings of those children, correctly. They should be able to know, even from an early age, the temperaments of the children in their care as well as their talents. The teachers should be able to discern and know which gifts are placed upon each child and should fast and pray before coming to teach so that the Holy Spirit can reveal the gifts and talents within each child.

2

Raising the
Dead Back to Life
CZ&CZ&

J esus Christ, our great example was in the business not only of healing the afflicted but that of resurrecting the dead back to life. In John 11:1-44, Jesus raised Lazarus back to life after four days in the grave. In Luke 7:11-17 the widow of Nain, whose only son, her only hope, died. But Jesus came and raised him back to life. Jarius' daughter was also raised back to life (Mark 5:27-43). During the period of Jesus' ministry, raising the dead was a common occurrence and the Word of God says that we too, will do great things. Amen.

Testimony of a Dead Man Raised in London

In April 2005, in the city of London, England, a very close relation of mine died of cancer of the throat at St.

Thomas Hospital. When I arrived at his room the relatives of the dead man were all gathered in the room saying farewell—crying and wailing, so I joined them in their grief.

After some time, one of the daughters of the dead man called me out to the corridor of the hospital. As we left the room and crossed the hall, I heard the Spirit of God say to me, "So Margaret, you do not even know who you are in the Lord, now go back to that room and lay your hand on the dead body and command life back to him." I ran as fast as I could back to the room and announced to everyone there that the Lord had told me that I should pray for the dead man.

Atheist Man Believed

There was a man, an atheist, who asked me why I had not come to the hospital and prayed for the man whilst he was still alive, and told me that it was too late to do so. I refused to listen to him and instead obeyed what the Lord had said to do, taking the anointing oil out of my bag and anointed the cold feet of the dead man.

Dead Man Raised

I raised my voice and prayed "Israel, I bind the spirit of death and hell over you right now and I release the Spirit of the living God upon your life in Jesus' name. Amen." This simple prayer took less than two minutes, after which I went to the corner of the room and knelt down praying in the Spirit.

Two minutes later, to the glory of the Lord, the dead man came back to life and was sat upon his bed in the hospital. There was stampede in the room, some people ran out shouting while others started cheering. The doctors and nurses in the wing came rushing in asking what was going on. When they came in and saw that the dead man had been resurrected they asked what I had done. I replied, simply, that I had prayed to my God—Jesus Christ.

The Power of Resurrection

The same man (the atheist) who had earlier challenged my praying for the dead man asked me how I had done this thing. I told him that it was done by the power of the Holy Ghost. God, beloved, has given us the authority in the name of Jesus, and He is expecting us to follow in His footsteps. Amen.

The dead man, who had not been able to eat for over three months, asked for water and soup. There is power in the Word of God, beloved. He is still healing people, still raising the dead today and forever more. Amen.

The Key to Raising The Dead Back to Life

By guiding my hands and my prayers toward John 11:1-44, where Lazarus is raised from the dead, the Holy Spirit had shown me the secret-key to raising the dead back to life.

Not By Our Hands But by His!

The first thing the Lord showed me was that whenever we, either believers or those of us in ministry lay our hands on to heal the sick, it is actually not our hands that heal, but the hands of the Lord. We are his instruments in this, and we should never be afraid to lay hands on the sick.

Jesus and the Father are one, as we are one with Jesus. When we offer up our hands, it's actually the hands and healing of the Lord that are being offered to the dying, the sick, and those demonically possessed. Remember that the Lord told us that He has delegated His power and authority to every believer to do even greater works than He did while on earth (John 14:12).

Reading the Story of Lazarus and Learning from the Lord

In John 11:3, Lazarus' sisters sent a message to the Lord that their only brother, a friend of Jesus', was sick. In verse 4 Jesus told His disciples that this sickness would not end in death, that instead the works of God's Son would be glorified through it. Amen.

Jesus told His disciples that his sickness "is not unto death but for the glory of God, that the Son of God may be glorified by it" [through His healing]. So: Saints of God, though today you may be going through some sickness of which doctors have given you an evil report or dire prognosis, remember the Word of God as demonstrated here—that these sicknesses are not unto death, but exist in order that the glory of God might be revealed.

Jesus did not rush to Martha and Mary for two days. In prayer we sometimes beg haste and crave immediacy. Sometimes God must delay in order to show forth His glory. He knows where you are and what succour you asked for and need, but He might delay so that the enemy may know that you serve an awesome God.

Jesus told his disciples, in verse 11, that their friend Lazarus had fallen asleep and said that he would journey there to bring him to wakefulness again. Today, by the same power and authority delegated to me, the Lord is going to wake-up every area of your life that is asleep in Jesus' name. Amen.

Jesus Spoke in Code to His Disciples

The disciples did not understand when Jesus said Lazarus was asleep—the sleep meaning—death. Jesus had to make his language plain enough that they could understand: LAZARUS IS DEAD. Before they arrived at the place where Lazarus lay buried, his sisters received the message that the Lord was on His way to see them. Today, even as you read this book I can share such a message with you: The Lord is on His way to see you and to meet every need that you have in Jesus' name. Amen.

Martha

When Martha heard that Jesus was on his way to them she ran to meet the Master and said to Him: Lord if only you had been here Lazarus would not have died, but I know that anything you ask of the Father He will do it.

Recognise, Saints, that the word, 'but' will rob us of the blessings, faith, healing and wonders that God wants to perform in our lives. The word, 'but' is a word every believer needs to extinguish from their thinking and speaking. Jesus, always perfect in His word said to Martha, "Your brother will rise again". Hallelujah! Amen.

Martha Had Not Yet Experienced the Revelation

Martha who still had not understood whom it was that stood before her, said, " I know that he will rise again, on the day of resurrection." Now Saints of God, let us hear this miraculous statement from the Word of the Lord:

"I am the resurrection and the life, He who believes in me will live, even though he dies, and whoever lives and believe in me will never die" (John 11:15).

Martha, Do You Believe?

Although Martha had stated that her brother would rise again on the day of resurrection, Jesus still had to ask Martha if she believed. Some of us, He knew, speak but do not truly believe that the words that we speak are Spirit and the life. Martha finally received the revelation and knew before whom she stood. 'Yes Lord', she said, 'I believe'. Martha then returned home and told her sister, Mary, that she has seen the Lord. Those of us who are saints and worshippers of the Lord can learn a valuable lesson in the difference between the reactions of the two sisters' regarding His coming.

Mary: My Kind of Woman

Martha was good and virtuous, but Mary's sorrow and humility were able to touch her Master's compassionate heart. In John 11:32, when Mary reached the place where Jesus was and saw him, she fell at His feet and spoke as her sister Martha had done: 'Lord, if you had been here, my brother would not have died'. The words of Mary's statement may have been the same as those of her sister's, but there was a difference between these two petitions. Mary fell at the feet of the Lord, just as she did before—when she poured expensive perfume on the Lord's feet wiping His feet with her hair.

Mary Weeping

When Jesus saw Mary weeping, He was touched and moved in the Spirit to act. If you wish to see the compassion of God, go to him like Mary— weeping and tears rolling down your face and in supplication. The Lord is moved, by your suffering because Jesus does not want to see any of his children weeping. He is a God of compassion and mercy. Today, Jesus is going to move on your behalf to remove every reproach from you in Jesus' name. Amen. The question that Jesus did not ask Martha, He then asked of Mary; where her brother was buried.

Jesus Wept

In John 11:35, Scripture shows us that Jesus wept. What a love He has for His children. So much so that he is weeping for us. Jesus was deeply moved by seeing Mary crying alongside all the other mourners. Martha again said when she heard that Jesus was asking where Lazarus was laid reminding Martha, "Did I not say that if only you believe early on, that you will see the glory of the Lord"? Then Jesus, the giver of life said to them, 'roll away the stone'. Hallelujah! Amen.

Roll Away the Stone

Today the Lord is rolling away every stone that the enemy has used to bury your ministries, your churches, your temples, your businesses and homes, your marriage, children, wombs, and anything else that is precious to you, in Jesus' name. Amen. The breath of God is here to raise everything that is dead in Jesus' name. Amen.

Remember the first message the Holy Spirit gave me, that Jesus and the Father are one, just as the Bible teaches. In John 11: 41 Jesus gave thanks to the Father and said that He knew His Father always heard him. This is a powerful statement and promise. Jesus was saying the same thing to the church of God; that if only we believe that He is the life and the resurrection then we can—by His grace and power—partake in even more miracles than the Lord Himself did when He was here on earth.

Lazarus Come Forth

Jesus called out with a loud voice: 'LAZARUS COME FORTH'. When the spirit of death and hell heard the voice of the one that created Lazarus, it had no choice but to let him go— once Jesus commanded that the grave clothes be removed release Lazarus. Today as a prophet of the living God, I call forth every dead area of your life to come forth now in Jesus' name. Amen.

Actions Begin

First the stone was rolled away from the tomb. Then Jesus commanded those gathered 'round to remove the grave cloth still laid on Lazarus and then, finally, Jesus said to let him go. God is going to do the same for you as He did for Lazarus in Jesus' name.

From today onward, your destinies are loosed, your virtues and all the dead churches and ministries are loosed and made to be as God intended. Our bodies are freed from sickness. Dead marriages and dead wombs will begin to bring forth life again, in Jesus' name. Amen.

This is the message every believer needs to hear and understand: The Holy Spirit wants to impart some blessings and revelations to us—His children.

Within the Spirit the number four means new beginning and life. On the fourth day of Lazarus's death

Jesus raised him up, on the fourth day of my 'Daniel fast' the Lord brought me this message to share with his children: Enjoy and believe to have the faith of God. Amen.

God Wants to Heal You Today

Beloved, are you in need of healing in any part of your body? Then place your right hand on that part of your body, now. If only you will believe you will see that greater things happen in your bodies.

> Father, in the name of Jesus! You are the great physician. Lord, we call upon your name to heal the reader of this book—who is trusting in you for divine healing in the name of Jesus. Lord, heal every hurt and wound they have carried. In Psalm 147:3 your Word says, "The Lord healeth the broken in heart, and mended their wounds".

May all your hurts be healed in Jesus' name! Amen.

Ability to Hear from God

One of the greatest, most glorious things to have within a ministry is the ability to hear the voice of God. The deceased man whom God resurrected through me could have been buried had the Holy Spirit not spoken to me and had I not, by the grace of God, had the ability to recognise the voice of the Holy Spirit. The spirit of fear could have prevented me from acting upon the voice of God by saying, 'What if this is not God, or what will people say if he does not rise up from the dead'? Let us have a child's purity of faith and act when God commands us. Amen.

Three Types of Voices

There are three types of voices. The first is the voice of God, secondly, the voice of Satan, and third—the voice of self. The Bible says that the sheep hear the voice of the Shepherd and the voice of another they will not follow. May we be able to hear the voice of God always and not of Satan, in Jesus' name! Amen.

Lastly, when we hear the voice of God we must act upon it and not delay. In delay we find doubt and uncertainty, the voices of self, and Satan—crowding out the Word of God. Amen

Prayer Points

O God Arise, release your healing oil upon your children now, in the name of Jesus.

You, spirit of cancer, I bind you right now in Jesus' name. Amen.

Thou healing power of God, arise and deliver your children now in Jesus' name. Amen.

Jesus, you are the Balm of Gilead. Heal all those who are calling upon you now in Jesus' name. Amen.

3

Healing the
Broken Hearted

CႽჀCႽჀ

In Psalm 147:3 the Word of God says:

"The Lord healeth the broken in heart and mends their wounds".

Naming a Ministry

In 2004 July, when the Lord gave me the name of the ministry, He said to me: "Daughter, close your eyes and imagine round the world how many people are crying and weeping right now calling upon me."

The Spirit of the Lord said to me: "How many people for various reasons round the world are now weeping, their hearts broken? I am sending you to them to comfort and deliver them from their pain. There are many people who are passing through the travails of life with broken hearts, some through marital distress, some whose businesses have fallen through, some through illness; there are so many reasons," the Lord said.

Be Encouraged

Whatever the reason that your heart is broken and in pieces, you are going to be encouraged and lifted in your spirit as you read the following testimonies, beloved. Amen. In Jeremiah 29 verse 11 the word of God says: "For I know the plans I have for you, says he Lord. They are plans for good and not for disaster, to give you a future and a hope". Amen.

We already know that God's plan for our lives are plans for good and not for evil. Anything outside of the bounds of good does not come from God but the ill will and evil actions wrought by the enemy.

Personal Testimonies

Beloved, I would like to share my testimony with you so that it may help to lift you out of your present situation. I pray that God will minister to you through this testimony of mine, in Jesus' name. Amen.

My Arrival in the United Kingdom

I came to London in my late teens after I left secondary school in Nigeria, to join my former husband. I got married early in life and I was not saved. In fact was not 'born again' at all. I was a nominal Christian who was brought up attending Catholic Church in Nigeria.

Upon my arrival in London, where I had come to join that husband, the difference between what I had expected and what I was met with was a great shock and a startling, devastating and violent surprise. The Bible tells us if the foundation is destroyed, what can the righteous do. That day—my very first day in a new country having travelled from Nigeria to London,— I was greeted by a middle-aged woman when we got to my new home.

My then-husband told me not to worry about her and that she was moving out the very next day. I asked him who the lady was. Only to be told that she used to be his girlfriend but that she had refused to move out of the house.

Disaster Starts

The first week in my husband's house quickly turned into a nightmare as this other woman became verbally and physically abusive toward me. The last straw came one evening when I walked into the living room. She rushed after me with a bottle of brandy and tried to hit me in the

41

head. God saved me as my husband quickly took the bottle from her hand, forcing her to leave soon after. Nonetheless, as I said earlier, the foundation of the relationship was already faulty.

I was so afraid. Imagine an inexperienced, naïve girl who was supposed to be enjoying her honeymoon but found such a life waiting for her instead. This marriage I would refer to as a union from the pit of hell. But God had his hand upon me even though I did not know Him then. I was blessed with three children, but the relationship was marked by beatings—my arm being broken, and the other women he brought into our matrimonial home including the various children he sired outside of our marriage.

Eventually, the betrayal that finally broke our marriage my husband told me that he was going to Nigeria to buy a house for the family and asked me to help him to borrow money from the bank. Thinking that I was helping him and my children to build a future, I agreed. Instead, he took that money and although he bought the property in Nigeria, he used the remaining money to marry another woman whom he brought back with him to London, to the home we shared.

His intention at the time, it turned out, was to live with two women in the same house! I had never seen anything like it before and I lacked the advice of more-experienced women who could offer me sound counsel. My three young children were exposed to these traumas and my own suffering upset them even more.

A Stranger in Our Home

Upon my husband's return, new wife in tow, I was put aside and treated like a second- class citizen—a house girl, in my own home. Soon this strange woman had taken over the matrimonial bedroom that my husband and I had shared, and I was sleeping in another room. A few months later, when I was only twenty-nine years old, the marriage was over.

A Wounded Heart

Beloved, what can such a wounded heart do? What can such a broken heart do? What can someone who has gone through such mental distress do? If Jesus Christ—our Rock—is absent from life and a marriage, then that marriage is doomed: A marriage without Jesus, a life without Jesus—is crisis.

When we go through life without proper counsel and guidance then we carry the baggage of our past into other relationships. The purpose of sharing these personal testimonies is to encourage you, to tell you that no matter how far you have gone, no matter how shattered your dreams are and no matter how broken you are, our God is still able to reach out in love to you and bring His restoration into your life.

Recover Before Entering into Another Relationship

I believe I was not totally healed from the relationship when I jumped into another in the name of Christianity. Shortly after the relationship with my first husband ended, someone introduced me to a man who at the time was living in Nigeria. Again, this man had an ulterior motive— his being that he was marrying me—to obtain settlement in the United Kingdom.

Under the Guise of Christianity

This new man in my life deceived me into believing he was a believer (a wolf in sheep's clothing). But I soon found out that he had offered me nothing but lies and deception—under the pretence of being a genuine Christian. It is only God, beloved, who knows who is serving Him in truth and spirit. When I got married the second time, I thought I was marrying a believer and that he would not treat me like my first husband. But sadly, I was tragically mistaken. Unbeknownst to me he had only wanted to marry because he knew that it would enable him to secure for himself a British citizenship.

Once he had secured his British passport, he packed up his things and moved out of the house. After spending my

44

time, my love and my money to help train him at a higher institution, helped him to renovate his home in Nigeria and set-up some businesses, and even helped to bury his mother, it turned out that he was another shark, another servant of the enemy and I was left completely shattered.

Suicidal Thoughts

It was at this point, after a second devastating betrayal, that I began to think of ending my life. I felt that my life was worthless, hopeless and that my very existence was pointless, that I should drive my car into London's Thames River and be done with. By this time my self-worth was gone, my self-confidence reduced to nothing— to rags and tatters. In order to keep me down and to keep me subservient to him, my second husband had told me repeatedly how ugly I was. Additionally, my business at that time had collapsed leaving me in debt— beside the money that he had taken from me.

Spiritual Blindness

Beloved, Satan will bring wrong and wicked people into one's life if we are blind spiritually, as I was then. I did not understand why I was suffering so, going through that hell right here on earth. Then, beloved, a fateful day came on which I planned to take my own life. Nothing seemed worth living for, not even my beautiful children with whom God had blessed me.

Suicidal Plans

On the day I planned to kill myself the Lord sent a man of God all the way from Uganda to save me. This man of God later told me that the Lord had told him to go to London, even described my woes to him and had shown him my face in a prophetic image. There was a Ugandan woman, a servant of God with whom and in whose house I used to go and pray, and unknown to me, this man of God had come to her house during the night vigil. This man of God, who had come so far to find me, described to her what the Lord had shown him. My friend knew immediately that the person—that the man of God had been sent to save—was me. So she immediately sent for me.

God of Intervention

By the time I got to the Ugandan woman's house I had broken down completely and wept non-stop for more than three-quarters of an hour. The servant of God was asking me what the matter was, but I could hardly talk or even open my mouth. With anger in his spirit, he got up from where he was sitting and came and laid his hand on my chest, crying: "Lord, heal this broken heart"! I fell down immediately and laughed for over 10 minutes. By the time I got up on my feet, it appeared and felt as though God had completely wiped away the memory of my pain, leaving me new and full of life.

The pastor from Uganda then called me, 'sister' and told me that the Lord had brought him there because of me. He said that God had told him that the journeys of my life were a testing ground, a training ground for the path ahead of me. He then took his anointing oil and poured it into my head, saying, "When Kish lost his asses and sent out Saul to go look for them and he came to Samuel the prophet and upon getting there, Samuel told Saul that the assess has been found and that Saul was going to be the next king of Israel, Samuel took his oil and anointed Saul".

Anointed Prophet

The man of God took his oil and anointed me and told me God was going to use me to minister to those who were hurting and in the same place where I had been comforted, God was going to use me to comfort others. He then told me that God was going to use me all around the world as His mouthpiece, as a prophet to nations.

God Is Not Looking for Perfect Vessels

Beloved of the Lord, I shared some of my trials in life with

47

you— the reader of this book— in order to encourage and reassure you that God is not looking for a perfect vessel to use. God is looking for broken vessels; those that are down and out, those society has deemed as outcasts; the rejected, the unknown, and the battered. God is not looking for perfect woman or man; he is only looking for those who are willing and available for his use.

He is looking for those who are hungry for Him, those who are thirsty for Him, so that He can give them the living water only Christ can provide. God wants to use the vessels that are empty so that He can fill them up to overflowing. Out of your overflow, people will come to partake of your oil because it is in this overflow that God shows His all. Today, I can truly testify about the goodness of the Lord in my life and ministry.

Divine Connection with Dr. D.K. Olukoya

In 2004, I was given the telephone number of Dr. D.K. Olukoya, the General Overseer of Mountain of Fire and Miracles Ministries Worldwide, based in Lagos, Nigeria. The lady who had given me Dr Olukoya's contact number told me that she had tried without success, for over six months to get in touch with the general overseer, and wished me luck. I thanked her and took the number. Later that night I prayed to the Lord: "Lord, you own the airwaves. Lord let Dr Olukoya answer this call." The phone rang just once beloved, just once before Dr Olukoya picked up the call. I was so shocked I started screaming and he gently said to me, "Sister, calm down and tell me what you want to ask the Lord to do for you".

He asked me if the number I was calling from was my own and said that he would go and pray for a day and a night before calling me back. True to his word, exactly twenty-four hours later, Dr Olukoya called me back from Lagos. Thank God that there are still true men of God!

Dr Olukoya, to whom I had told nothing about myself— or my life, gave me the counsel and the Word of God. The first thing he did was to ask me what I did for a living. I replied that I was a social worker and also a businesswoman. He then floored me with a question: "Is that what God called you to do?" He asked me if I had known that I was born a billionaire despite my life not then reflecting it and that my largess and generosity, the charity I would do in God's holy name would be humbling to kings.

⚜︎❧⚜︎❧⚜︎

Deliverance at Mountain of Fire and Miracles Ministries

Dr Olukoya asked if I was able to travel out of the country, which my British Passport let me do and suggested that I came for deliverance in Nigeria, where he would help conduct my religious emancipation and unlock the gifts and talents that the Lord—by his grace and kindness had given me. I did not know anyone in Lagos, but Dr Olukoya, true to his kind nature, offered to put me up at the church's guesthouse. I immediately proceeded to Lagos to meet Dr Olukoya to commence the deliverance.

On the third day of my deliverance in Prayer City, Lagos, the Lord appeared to me at 1.30am on the 13th July 2004 and spoke to me the name of our ministry. The Lord said to me "Daughter, the name of your ministry is to be: "The Broken Hearted Ministries." At the time, I actually laughed, and asked the Lord why he had chosen that name for our ministry. The Lord said to read Psalm 147:3 and when I opened my Bible in the night I found that the Word of the Lord provided answers: The Lord healeth the broken in heart and mended their wounds.

The Lord then told me to close my eyes, to try and imagine His entire world and how many people were crying and weeping at that very moment. He told me that that was how big my ministry was to be, that the ministry would be a worldwide ministry and a healing ministry, attending to and caring for those who are hurting and wounded in their hearts.

Birthing of the Broken Hearted World Outreach Ministries

The ministry was born on the 13th of July 2004 in

Lagos, Nigeria when the Lord said to me, "Daughter, go as my mouthpiece and as my prophet to nations of the world, healing and delivering and bringing back my lost sheep."

As you read this book, God wants to restore your broken heart. God wants to bring deliverance to you. Beloved, what our Lord did for me by sending me a man of God during my time of distress, He wants to do for you now.

God Is No Respecter of Persons

Remember that God is not a respecter of persons, and that what He did for me He will do for you if only you will weep sincerely and freely in front of the Lord and completely surrender your will and your fate to Him. This is what I did when my entire world collapsed, when I could not see my way out of strife and misery, but supplication can be an act of love, a choice, rather than the default of despair.

Weep No More Beloved

I do not know what issues you might be going through but I bring a word from the Lord directly to you— my beloved. The Lord said to tell you to weep no more my beloved, to arise and to shine, for your light has come (Isaiah 60:1). There is hope for your future says the Lord. Your children will come again to their own land (Jeremiah 31:17). Amen.

51

❊⤲⤳❊❊⤲⤳❊
God Will Send You a Deliverer

Beloved, if God can cause a pastor whom I had never met and had no connection to journey all the way from Uganda for my sake then know as a certainty that God will bring someone to come and bless you. Amen. The Lord who rose up mightily, the man of God—Dr Olukoya for my sake, will offer the same blessings and succour to you right now. You did not buy this book by chance or by accident, you are feeling the hand of the Holy Spirit guiding you and acting upon His Divine will.

This book is written with a hand guided entirely by that divinity to bring you hope and the expectation of abounding happiness and peace under God's attentive and loving gaze. The earthly father I did not have, God raised Dr Olukoya to be that father and leader whom I so desperately needed in those darker seasons of my life.

❊⤲⤳❊❊⤲⤳❊
The Blessed Mentorship of Dr. D.K. Olukoya

Dr. Olukoya has nurtured and groomed me with his leadership style. His much-needed and eternally appreciated fatherly support and courage has added value to my life and ministry. He is truly a leader of God's people, mighty in intellect, always eager for the things of God, an apostle of brokenness; a visionary leader who is tender in spirit and warm in affection. He is truly my mentor in this earthly life.

Dr Olukoya has taught me to believe that I can make it in life and ministry as a woman by the act of prayer warfare and through the worth and glory to God my ministry can provide. I salute you Dad and may Almighty God continue to guide and protect you in Jesus' name. Amen.

God Wants to Give You a Second Chance

Beloved, today, I thank God for my second chance. He has restored my joy and my hope. Where the enemy intended evil for me, God turned into good for my sake. My prayer for you as you read this book is that God will restore you, restore all the years that the locusts have eaten. God will restore joy and happiness into your life again in Jesus' name. Amen.

The Word of God says that looking unto God, the Author and the Finisher of our faith, you can hold on, be strong and be courageous. God has not forgotten you.

O Lord Heal My Broken Heart and Infirmities

Isaiah 53:5
"But He was wounded for our transgressions, He

was bruised for our iniquities; the chastisement for peace was upon Him; and by His stripes we were healed".

Psalm 147:3
"He heals the broken hearted and binds up their wounds".

Prayer Points

O Lord, I thank you for your mercy that has kept me all these years in the name of Jesus.

O Lord, thank you for healing my broken heart and mending my wounds in the name of Jesus.

O Lord, thank you for your unconditional love toward me in the name of Jesus.

O Lord, I thank you in the name of your Son Jesus for restoring all the years that the locusts and the caterpillars devoured.

O Lord, thank you for giving me a second chance to be used of thee in the name of Jesus.

O Lord, by your power, I am moving forward in my God-ordained destiny in the name of Jesus.

O Lord, use me now for your glory in Jesus' name.

4

About
The Vision
CR8OCR8O

A Call To Gather Women...

A Call to Gather Women to Pray and Fast for the UK and
Nigeria

Beloved, toward the end of my forty days of marathon dry
fasting and waiting on the Lord in 2009, the Spirit of the
Lord spoke to me and told me to go and lead women of all
ages, regardless of their denominations, creed, colour and
churches to pray over the nations of the United Kingdom
and Nigeria.

The Lord said that on that day of prayer all women
old and young will come together to fast and pray for the
glory of God to come back to these nations. The Lord told to

me we need prayers of repentance and for the forgiveness of sins. We should lift these nations before the Lord and ask for the fresh fire of God over the land. The Lord said that we should cry aloud for the glory and fire of revival to come back to the nations of the United Kingdom and Nigeria.

My response was to say to the Lord that we already have a global day of prayer for the UK, but the Spirit of God chastened me and said that women are the ones who carry spiritual wombs and would birth forth the revival in these nations.

Aims and Objectives

Prayer of repentance for the sins of our forefathers

Spiritual cleansing of the nations

Prayer to remove curses from the lands

Prayer for restoration over the nations

Prayer for revival and the fresh fire of God

Prayer for the breath of God to come back to the nations

Gathering of Women

The Lord said to gather women to arise and bid them to travel to the places of prayer. The mandate of God is simple: Gather women of all ages and arise as a mighty army for the

Lord.

The Deborah's and Esther's of Our Generation

God is raising the Deborah's and the Esther's of our generations to help to repair and to rebuild the walls of these nations. Wherever you are you women of God, the Lord is calling you to rise up to help rebuild the walls of your various nations like Nehemiah did in rebuilding the walls of Jerusalem (Nehemiah 3).

Women, God is saying that this is our time; this is the moment in which we can birth nations through our prayers, revivals and re-awakenings. God is counting upon us to arise and take our rightful places in prayer and travail; birthing that which God has already planted inside of us. Amen.

Beloved women of God, when there was a need in the land of Israel, Deborah arose and led the nation. Today, there is a need to come together and pray for our various nations that God has placed us in. Arise and don't accept any claims that you are weaker vessels, but gird yourselves—mighty women of God—and move! Do mighty exploits for my kingdom saith the Lord of Hosts.

Esther Coming into the Kingdom

In the Book of Esther (3:13-16) this is essentially what

57

happened: Mordecai sent this reply to Esther; don't think for a moment that because you are in the palace you will escape when all other Jews are killed. If you keep quiet at a time like this, deliverance and relief for the Jews will arise from some other place, but you and your relatives will die, who knows if perhaps you were made queen for such a time as this?

Then Esther sent this reply to Mordecai: Go and gather all the Jews of Susa and fast for me. Do not eat or drink for three days, night and day. My maids and I will do the same. And then, though it is against the law, I will go in to see the king. If I must die, I must die.

Arise Mighty Women

Women from all walks of life: God has raised you for such a time as this! Let us stand up and fight for our future, the future of our as yet unborn children. God is counting on us. Amen.

Then Deborah Arose: A Judge and a Prophet

Another story of a brave woman is that of Deborah from Judges 4:5, a Prophetess, a wife and judge of Israel—the only woman to hold that office. Under her guidance, Barak conquered Sisera and delivered Israel from the oppression of the Canaanite, King Yavin. She served as Israel's judge when no men were willing to lead and unite the people of

58

Israel, bringing peace to the land under her leadership for 40 years. Deborah was a judge and a prophetess, and she was one of the five women in the bible called a "prophet". The triumphant song of Deborah is one of the most ancient literary pieces in the Bible.

Peace in Our Lands and Nations

Daughters of Zion! God wants to bring His peace to our various lands and nations, hence the call to arise and pray. Are you the Deborah and Esther of your nation? Rise up and be counted. Amen.

5

How to Hear
from God Dreams
ᏨᏦᎧᏨᏦᎧ

There are various ways in which God communicates with us, although a great number of people do not know or understand when God is trying to speak with them, when in fact God uses over thirty-known methods to share His Grace, His Wisdom and His Will with us.

God speaks to us individually and asks us to share his messages from person to person. As believers, it is important to recognise which method the Lord uses to communicate with us, so that we might recognise our callings and follow them in faith.

When God started communicating with me I was very young. I received some of his messages through dreams and my mother told me that even as a baby, I would often be the first person in the family to observe things which they had not yet observed.

Dreams from My Early Years

Once, during my early teens, I dreamt that my father—who is now no longer with us, was riding his motorcycle on his way home. In the dream I saw two very long trailers coming from a junction in the road and heading blindly—straight toward my father. To avoid being killed he had to steer his motorcycle into a ditch and I saw that although he had survived he was badly injured. When I awoke I was sweating and shaking.

I was not "born again" at this point in my life; hence I did not know how to stop this dream from coming to pass, so I turned to my mother. She, perhaps believing the dream to be a sign or perhaps trying to put my mind at ease, phoned my father and told him about my dream. That evening he decided to leave his motorcycle at work and got a lift home from a colleague.

Fulfilment of an Evil Dream

Two days later my father decided it was safe to ride his motorcycle home from work. At about 8 p.m. a police officer came to our house and informed us that my father had been involved in an accident involving two trailers and that he had had to jump into a ditch, exactly as the Lord had shown me prior to it happening. Later I came to understand that dreams are one of the ways God uses to talk or to reveal things to us.

Another dream was about a Nigerian plane crash. I told a friend of mine that I had a bad dream concerning a plane bearing the Nigerian flag that crashed in Nigeria. He said to me, 'God forbid'. I had this dream 5.30 a.m. and by 5 p.m. on the same day, sadly, it was reported that a Nigerian plane had crashed killing all the members on board.

Visions

God uses visions to communicate with us. A vision is like a dream—but it is vivid, strange and striking in character and in effect. Visions can happen in the night, as it did to Jacob in Beersheba Genesis 46:2 or by day, when the visionary is wide-awake.

Visitation from the Lord

When God's hand is upon us, many people start to receive regular visitations from the Lord. In the early days of my ministry I had several visitations from the Lord but, at first, I was too frightened to reveal these to anyone for fear of being labelled mad. I was having open visions, deep revelations, dreams, audible voice of God, but was too scared to let anyone know.

On one occasion I had a vision of the burning bush experience. I saw seven buses all lined up and I saw gouts of flames on their sides but they were not consumed. I wiped my eyes, scared that perhaps I was seeing things which were not of God or that I was losing my mind. Then I heard the Spirit of God say to me that that was a holy ground and made mention of the experience of Moses and the burning bush.

On yet another occasion, when I was working during the night, I was reading Pastor Benny Hinn's book, Good Morning Holy Spirit and thinking about the experience Pastor Benny Hinn had during his visit to one of Katherine Kulman's meetings. He saw the raw power of the Holy Ghost during that gathering and so I then had courage to speak to the Lord. I admitted that I did not yet know Him the way Pastor Benny Hinn was describing in his book and offering a fervent prayer that this might change: "My precious Holy Spirit, I want to experience you the way Benny Hinn did."

❊❧❦❊❦❧❊❊ Night of Divine Visitation

At about 1:30 a.m. I went upstairs to have my break at work and as I entered into the lounge area there was only one small chair and nothing else, I switched off the light so that no one could see me sleeping. As I moved toward the chair I suddenly sensed that there was something unusual about the room—some sort of presence or aura—but since I was the person who turned off the light and there was nobody else there I crossed over to the chair.

I sat down and stretched out my legs, resting my head on the chair. After a couple of minutes, I felt a hand lift my head up from the chair, I was scared and screamed the Lord's name.

I saw a Bible opened in front of me with red letters written in it, but I was too scared to read what the Lord was trying to show me. Immediately I felt as though I was being spun around and I started to speak in tongues. When I was released from this sensation, as abruptly as it had begun, I looked at the time. It was 4:30 a.m. and I had been speaking in "tongues" for nearly three hours. I was scared by the strength of the experience and could not share this experience with anyone at the time, except for the one person who was closest to me then.

A lot of people who are inexperienced in the things of God are seeing the Lord and hearing His voice but are not equipped or able to discern the significance or the import of the gift that is being given to them. In the Book of Luke Chapter 1 when the Archangel Gabriel visited Mary, the mother of Jesus, it was a visitation of the Lord in order to announce that the Virgin Mary would conceive and give birth to our Lord Jesus Christ.

Another person that the angel visited was Zechariah, the husband of Elizabeth, who was the mother of John the Baptist. He had a visitation of the Lord when he was in the temple and was told that his wife would conceived and give birth to a son named John—who would be the forerunner of Christ in bringing the Lord's salvation message (Luke 1:11-19.).

Divine Visitation of an Angel

In 2006, I was in Bible School in Fort Myers, Florida, when very early in the morning at about 5.30 a.m., after my night vigil, I saw an angel of the Lord come into my room. He had in his hand a measuring tape and told me that God wanted me to set-up an orphanage in Kogi State, Nigeria.

The land the angel measured out to me was over 6,000 square feet and I asked the angel where I would get such a parcel of land, given that I had left Nigeria over 29 years ago at the time. The angel said to me that it was the Lord's will and that He would bring it to pass.

Prophesy Fulfilled

Beloved, in February 2011, God brought His word to pass when the state government allocated to us large portions of land in Lokoja for the orphanage. The same week, his Royal Majesty, the Ohinozi of Ebira, donated land to the ministry (12.5 hectares) for the same orphanage along the Okene-Ajaokuta Road in Ajaokuta, Kogi State, Nigeria. When the Lord speaks, beloved, He always brings His will to pass. Amen.

Visions can come as revelations and prophecies and examples of both can be found in the Bible. In Daniel 7:8-10, Daniel received a vision in which the future of mankind and the end of all things were unveiled to him. John, the beloved apostle also had a vision in which a description of the troubled times ahead which would lead to the end of the world. Visions can be plain and direct at times, as in Genesis 15:1-4; Acts 9:10-19; Acts 10:3-6 and they can also be prophetic and arrive in the form of allegories (Jeremiah 24:1-10).

Open Visions

God sometimes speaks to his children through open-visions. This is a spiritual experience in which a person while conscious and wide-awake receives a message or sees a panorama of events or a vanishing view of an object. This form of vision can be short and transient. Open-visions share some similarities to open-trances.

Trance

Trance[s] is another method by which God speaks to mankind, a condition of partial consciousness or an absolute trance; visions are received and hallucinations experienced. In this condition, the Holy Spirit can impart God's message to a whole assembly of believers. In deliverance cases, an indwelling spirit may manifest and speak out, using the mouth of the person in the trance. A discerning listener will normally detect the nature of the manifesting spirit by the nature of the message spoken aloud.

Messages received through a trance are said to be plain when they are direct, or coded when they require interpretation. Examples of people who fell into a trance in the Bible include Peter, Acts 10:1 and Paul, Acts 22:17-18.

Open Trance

God also speaks to his followers through what is termed, an open-trance. As in an open vision, a person who falls into an open-trance may do so consciously with their eyes wide-open. However, an open-trance is longer in duration than an open-vision. A few seconds of experience may take much longer to describe verbally.

In the scripture, Balaam's blessing on the children of

68

Israel was received and delivered under the seizure of an open-trance; that is so say, he was in a prolonged trance with his eyes wide-open (Numbers 24:1-4). Joshua's encounter with the angelic commander of the Lord's army was also in an open-trance (Joshua 5:13-16).

Another instance of open-trance was the message, which an angel of God delivered to Daniel after 21 days delay in the heavenlies (Daniel 10:7-8). It is important to note that the trance was so protracted that it took Daniel three chapters of his book to relate the details of the encounter (Daniel 10:12).

Audio Channels

There are three types of audible channels by which God can speak. They are the small still voice, the voice at the back of the ears (the audible voice of God), and thunder.

1. A Small Still Voice

An example of this can be found in the first Book of Kings 19:12-13 when Elijah heard as God spoke to him with a small still voice. A lot of people hear this still small voice of God but, sadly, many of them are unable to recognise who is talking to them.

2. Hearing at the Back of the Ears

A typical example of this can be found in 1 Samuel 3:3-10. When Samuel first heard the voice of the Lord in the temple, he rushed to Eli's bedchamber. He was certain he had heard a voice call his name and thought it must have been from Eli. Since messages from the Lord were very rare in those days, Eli assumed that Samuel had simply misheard some other noise, and it took three such calls for Eli to realize that God wanted to speak to Samuel.

Hearing at the back of my ears has been central to my life's work. In one memorable instance I was living in London when the Lord told me to move back to Nigeria, having left there to settle in the UK thirty-one years previously— in order to strengthen the hands of women and children and be a voice to the nation. The Lord said to go back to the country of my birth and that he would establish me there.

In 2010 I had another experience of the audible voice of God after I asked the Lord to appear to me, His servant. I went to sleep that night and at about 1.30 a.m. I heard a call which felt as though someone had put a speaker to my ear and shouted my name through it. It continued: "Margaret, stand up onto your feet, your Maker wants to speak with you." This is similar to what happened to Prophet Ezekiel in the Book of Ezekiel 2 verse 1-2. I was shocked, beloved, and terrified by the realisation of my own presumption in asking the Lord to appear to me, but the Lord spoke to me about the ministry and the life that awaited me.

3. Thunder

In the encounter at Mount Sinai, the children of Israel had to plead with God to stop speaking to them because they feared that the volume of His thundering voice would kill them (Exodus 20:18-19; Deuteronomy 5:24-27).

Meditation

Another path by which God can speak to His children is through our practice and use of meditation. God imparts profound knowledge and privileged information to people who meditate deeply in His word (Psalm 119:99). He loves to inspire people. He loves to sharpen their vision and imagery and delights in showing them something new—even more so when their minds are absorbed in deep reflection—in a quiet place or serene environment.

Many men and women of God have received inspiring messages from the Lord whilst meditating on the Word or just having their quiet contemplation in His name and presence. The Bible says that those who meditate on the Word of God daily will receive great insight, understanding and prosperity: Joshua 1:8; Ezra 3:3; Psalm 1:1-3; Jeremiah 1:16.

Perception

God speaks to people through the gift of perception allowing them to see through their soul's insightful eyes or giving them knowledge through their soul's perfect senses. Perception enables someone to recognise and understand something that has not yet been revealed or to see with one's inner-eye an event that has not yet come to pass. In Psalm 139:1-2 the Word of God says: "O Lord, you have searched me and you know me. You know when I sit and when I rise; you perceive my thoughts from afar".

An example of such divine perception is found in John 4:19, when the Samaritan woman at Jacob's well said to Jesus, "Sir, I perceive that you are a prophet".

The Spoken Word of God (Rhema)

One powerful way by which God speaks to His children is through the rhema, when the written word strikes the heart first, then keeps repeating itself to the receiver sticking in their heart and finally keeps burning in them (Jeremiah 20: 9).

Discernment of Spirit

This is the supernatural power of seeing into the spirit realm and detecting the operational gift in a person or location. It is God's way of passing information to His children about the nature of a stranger or the state of an unfamiliar environment. As a matter of fact, there have been instances where we have warned some of our members not to rent or buy particular properties because of the prevalence of demonic influences in those places.

The example of this happened when I was on my way to Nigeria in year 2009. I met an elderly gentleman travelling on the same flight as myself. As soon as I saw him, I was able to discern that he was going to be attacked by armed robbers on his trip. I was able to warn him and God used that warning to save his life. This elderly man was indeed attacked by a gang of armed robbers on that same trip but the Lord spared his life.

Gifts of Faith

God speaks to us through the gift of faith. This is the ability to believe God without hesitation (1 Corinthians 2:9). This type of faith goes beyond natural faith or saving faith. It is a special kind of faith that can move mountains (Matthew 17:19-20; 1 Corinthians 13:2b).

It enables the gifted person to walk by faith and not by sight—to believe in God's Word above the evidence of the senses, knowing that natural circumstances can be shaped or modified by the Word of God (2 Corinthians 5:7).

An example of this gift of faith manifested in my life in April 2005, when I heard the Lord say to me that I should go and lay hands on the dead man. I acted in faith and laid hands on him and prayed. To the glory of God, the dead man came back to life just as instructed by the Lord.

Word of Wisdom

Sometimes God speaks to his children through a Word of Wisdom (1 Corinthians 12:8). A Word of wisdom is a message given through the Holy Spirit divinely disclosing the mind, the purpose, and the way of God for a specific situation. It is a counsel deep in understanding and judgment, guidance acute in prudence and foresight.

Deborah gave Barak a word of wisdom when he declined to go to war unless she went with him. Deborah said, "Very well, I will go with you. But since you have made this choice, you will receive no honour. For the Lord's victory over Sisera will be at the hands of a woman" (Judges. 4:9). And so it was that Jael, the wife of Heber the Kenite, received greater military glory than Barak, when she hacked Sisera to death (Judges 4:17-22).

Word of Knowledge

The Lord also speaks through the Word of knowledge, a revelation of facts or a disclosure of confidential information on a particular person, matter, or event for the purpose of enlightenment. Also, by a Word of knowledge, the divine will and plan can be revealed to the faithful without the assistance of any human investigation or resource.

✻❦❧✻❦✻❦❧✻
A Samaritan Woman's Encounter

There is a Biblical example in the Book of John when Jesus released a Word of knowledge to the Samaritan woman beside Jacob's well: "You have well said, I have no husband; for you have had five husbands; and the one whom you now have is not your husband, in that you spoke truly."

The woman rushed back to her people saying, come and see the man who told me all things I ever did. Could this be the Christ (John 4:17-19)? In Acts 10, Peter received a word of knowledge from the Holy Spirit, saying, "Behold three men are seeking you – Arise therefore, go down and go with them. And Peter went down, found the visitors, and followed them to Caesarea without complaining" (Acts 10:19-23)

6

Wake-Up Sleeping Churches!

ᑕᔓᘰᑕᔓᘰ

In Esther 4:13-14: Mordecai sent this message to her: "I don't think for a moment that because you're in the palace you will escape when all other Jews are killed. If you keep quiet at a time like this, deliverance and relief for the Jews will arise from some other place but you and your relatives will die. Who knows, perhaps you were made queen for such a time as this?"

As a church, beloved, we need to:

Identify the times in which, we live.

Know how to respond appropriately.

Hear what the Holy Spirit is saying to the church.

Discover and create the new shape of the church.

Have an understanding of what the devil is trying to do and what aggressions he plans against our ministry in this time of change.

Learn how to survive in the days ahead.

✕❧✖✕❧✕
What Is the Lord Doing at This Time?

God is never taken unaware. It does not matter how dark the situation might seem. It does not matter if the devil has a plot. It does not matter how forlorn and hopeless or insurmountable a challenge might be because God is still in charge and He is not short of ideas or strategies. Those strategies may not be too clear to us, God's instruments may not be known to mortal man, yet God is still and always will be in control.

Pastors and church leaders—we must keep calm and spread this serenity to our congregations. Let us be confident in the assurance that God is totally in control and that He alone will have the final say regarding the fate of nations.

God always uses the most unusual people—the down and outs and the rejected, the broken and the despised, the unqualified and those without platforms or grand titles, in order to carry out his divine purpose. These instruments of

God's glory and power will be the nobodies. They will be men and women who have been called insignificant, raised from obscurity with no known backgrounds of which to speak.

The Days of the Super Heroes Are Over

The church in this season has been raised by God and positioned for this moment. Even though there are spiritual conspiracies, God has already positioned the faithful remnant. Just as Esther, an insignificant and unknown woman, she was placed at the most strategic place by the Lord's will. So too, are we readied for such a time. These remnants are the unnamed, the faceless, with no ministerial titles to their names; this is what is referred to as the Esther church, beloved.

These seemingly unimportant figures will not belong to the big cycle of ministers; their names have never been seen or heard. They are the Elijah's of this season: they will change destinies. These are going to be the shapers of nations.

Many of these remnants will not have had training in big Bible schools or seminaries, but these are going to be people who have passed through the wilderness, armoured in their faith. These people are those who have been tested and are awaiting—their hour of their glory.

How Will the New Churches that Emerge from These Dead Churches Survive in the Perilous Times Ahead?

God is the one who can lift nations up but also bring them down if they fail to obey His commandments. In James 1:17, we learn that every good and perfect gift is from above. One might think that the appointment of Esther was a coincidence, but in the plans of God, He, who orders our steps—there can be no coincidences. God is also the one who chooses a nation to favour, chooses which leaders will serve in His name and for His Glory.

The Word of God tells us that the heart of the king is in the hand of the Lord, He turneth it wheresoever He desires. Whenever God wants to bless us, or promote or honour a person or a nation, He will grant them favour as God granted Nehemiah favour before the king (Nehemiah 2:15). God is the only giver of favour, and will only grant His favour to those who love and worship him. Esther received favour from the Lord because of His mercy, grace and the works in which she was to play a part.

Our God is a faithful God. He keeps his covenant and will always make sure that the plan of the enemy is brought to nothing. All those who are planning to silence the voice of Christianity in this nation and other nations should learn from what happened to Haman and his plan to destroy the Jews. Anti-Semitism is an age-old volatile problem.

In Isaiah 54:15, the Word of God says: "Behold they

shall surely gather, but not by me, whosoever shall gather for our sake shall fall for thy sake." Amen. Haman paid a large sum of money into the king's treasury in order to have all the Jewish subjects killed. Do not be deceived beloved, the enemy will stop at nothing to try to destroy Christianity and I sincerely believe that the plan of the enemy is to stifle the churches of Europe and other nations and to stop the spread of Christianity.

What Are the Areas on Which We Need to Focus Our Prayers?

Marriage Christian principles to be taught in schools and the establishment of more Christian schools.

Stop the pollution of the next generation through withdrawing the sex education in early years children, in the media and schools.

God will have the final say in the affairs of all the nations of the world. He is going to raise unusual and unlikely people, the rejected and the disenfranchised, to carry out His work.

※ᘒᕉᘒᕉ※ᘒᕉ※

It Is Time for Our Churches to Awaken from its Spiritual Sleep

Just as God used Mordecai to awake Esther up from her sleep I believe, with all my heart, that God is raising the Esther Church of our generation to wake us up from our spiritual sleep, slowly. The churches have been fast asleep while the enemy was planning, but it has come time for us to wake-up.

Esther 4:10-11: Esther was given reasons why she might die, because the king had not sent for her. Esther forgot that God planted her in the palace for a time such as this and Mordecai had to wake her from her sleep and confront her with the reality of what was about to happen to the Jews.

Mordecai had to awaken Esther to her calling and assignment. My Lord! How we need the Mordecai of our times to wake-up the dead churches that are fast asleep. WAKE-UP!

The Lord Is Sounding His Trumpet Call

In Deuteronomy 6:10-12 God is warning us to be careful, to be guarded against being carried away by the god of mammon. God is warning us to be alert, so that we will not follow the false gods of this world. Many believers have become faint-hearted, they have stopped fasting and praying, stopped giving and have lost their passion for the work of God. Lord, have mercy upon our nations and heal our lands.

Many people are fast asleep in the lap of Delilahs; some nations have become graveyards to the people who came to the country hot in their pursuits of God but have waxed cold, a gross darkness upon the land. God wants the light brought back to these and all nations. The Lord is calling upon all the churches to fast and pray for our various nations. Esther 4:15-16, Esther declared three days and nights of fasting and prayers and now we need to do likewise, crying unto the Lord for forgiveness and repentance of our sins so that the Lord will hear us from heaven and heal our lands.

> 2 Chronicles 7:14-15:
> "If my people who are called by my name will humble themselves and pray and seek my face, and turn from their wicked ways, then I will hear from heaven and forgive their sins, and will heal their lands. Now mine eyes shall be opened, and mine ears attend unto the prayer that is made in this place."

Lord, I pray that all the churches of Christ; the Baptists, Anglicans, Methodists, etc. will come together and pray—seeking the face of the Lord for their nations so that a reawakening will sweep the world. We cry out to the Lord for a fresh rain over our nations! Let us petition Heaven and God will hear our sincere heart cry again.

Prayer Points

We need to pray against the enemy's plans to kill our faith.

We need to pray that the Lord will rouse us as a church so that the plans of the enemy will not come to pass.

We need to pray for reformers to be active in our various nations, for godly men and women to be raised up. These reformers will not sell-out our national birthrights; they will fear the Lord and speak the true voice of God in this dark season.

God wants us to rise up from our spiritual sleep and begin to pray fervently, never ceasing until we see a change come to our nations. Amen.

Suggested practical action:

Pray that every conspiracy of our enemy, Satan, is brought to nought like that of Haman.

Pray that God wakes-up the church so we can see the

schemes of the enemy to destroy our Judaeo-Christian values and also know how to respond appropriately.

Pray for reformers to become active in our various lands— Elizabeth Fry, John Howard and William Wilberforce and organisations such as the Clapham Sect.

Sound the Trumpet The Call of God to His Church

7

My Precious
Holy Spirit

CRBOCRBO

"Then he answered and spake unto me, saying, This is the word of the Lord unto Zerubbabel, saying, Not by might, nor by power, but by My Spirit, saith the Lord of Hosts". — Zechariah 4:6

This section of my book is dedicated to my precious Holy Spirit. From the time I was visited by the Holy Spirit in 2001, my life truly has never been the same. The joy of my newfound fellowship is beyond description.

Who Is the Person of the Holy Spirit?

- ⚘ The Holy Spirit is God.
- ⚘ The Holy Spirit is the executor or the Third Head.

- ✤ The Holy Spirit is God's executive agent on earth today.
- ✤ The Holy Spirit is the Spirit of the Father.
- ✤ The Holy Spirit is the one who searches all things (Romans 11:38).
- ✤ The Holy Spirit is the one who dwells with the saints (John 14:17).
- ✤ The Holy Spirit is the Creator and giver of life (Job 33:4.).
- ✤ The Holy Spirit is the one who glorifies Jesus Christ (John 16:14).
- ✤ The Holy Spirit is our teacher (John 14:26; 1 Corinthians 12:3).
- ✤ The Holy Spirit is the Helper of our infirmities (Romans 8:26).
- ✤ The Holy Spirit is the one who guides us (John 16:13).
- ✤ The Holy Spirit is the one present in the work of creation (Genesis 1:2).
- ✤ The Holy Spirit is the one that came upon Elijah (1 Kings 18:12).
- ✤ The Holy Spirit is the one who came upon Moses (Numbers 11:17).
- ✤ The Holy Spirit is the one who anointed the Saviour (Matthew 3:16; Luke 4:18).
- ✤ The Holy Spirit is the one who empowered the Saviour (Matthew 12:28).
- ✤ The Holy Spirit is the one who led the Saviour to

Calvary (Hebrews 9:14).

✤ The Holy Spirit is the one who directs the church's missionary work (Acts 8:29).

✤ The Holy Spirit is the one who gave birth to the church (Acts 2:1-4).

✤ The Holy Spirit is the one who appoints church ministers (1 Corinthians 2:4).

✤ The Holy Spirit is the one who baptises the believer (Romans 6:3-4).

✤ The Holy Spirit is the one who seals the believer (2 Corinthians 1:22).

✤ The Holy Spirit is the one who fills the believer (Acts 2:4).

✤ The Holy Spirit is the one who conforms believers to the image of Christ (2 Corinthians 3:18).

✤ The Holy Spirit is the one who instructs the ministers.

✤ The Holy Spirit is the voice of God instilled within   t h e   believer.

✤ The Holy Spirit is that one who sanctifies (Romans 15:16).

✤ The Holy Spirit is the one who reveals Biblical truth to believers (1 Corinthians 2:10).

✤ The Holy Spirit is the one who assures believers concerning their salvation   (Romans 8:16).

✤ The Holy Spirit is the one who imparts the love of Christ to believers and through believers Romans (5:5).

✍ The Holy Spirit is the one who will someday raise the bodies of all the departed believers (Romans 8:11).

The Holy Spirit is truly our Comforter and guide. Without His presence in the life of a believer, their journey walking a Christian path has yet to truly begin. The Holy Spirit is the one who brings the word of God alive in our hearts and ministries.

Each day when I wake up I whisper gently to my most precious Holy Spirit, telling Him how much He means to me. He is closer than the air I breathe-in. He is so real, beloved. He is more precious than any diamond or priceless object. He is the third person of the Trinity.

Precious Holy Spirit, I thank you for counting me worthy to be your friend; you are my senior partner in life and ministry. So many people have written books about the Holy Spirit, but none have truly touched and changed my life like the work of Pastor Benny Hinn, titled: Good Morning Holy Spirit.

The book that transformed my life about the Person of the Holy Spirit: Good Morning Holy Spirit.

Beloved, when I read this book I went onto my knees

and cried from the depth of my soul, saying" Holy Spirit, I really don't know you the way Pastor Benny Hinn has described you, but if truly you are real, tonight, make yourself known to me." That short prayer transformed me from the inside out. I bless the Lord for sending us The Holy Spirit of God, He is truly the greatest gift any believer could ever want or ask for. My personal walk with the Holy Spirit has changed my life and the lives of those around me. There is no way in which an individual's life, once they have welcomed the Holy Spirit into it, will not be changed in a real and tangible way.

Earlier, I shared my testimony about how I was spiralling into despair and destruction. Nonetheless, when the Holy Spirit entered into my life it brought true transformation with it. I lack the words to thank the precious Holy Spirit, because of His divine touch in my life I am now assured of my salvation and, by the grace of God, a candidate of heaven.

By the special generosity of God I am going to pass this flame of fire around the world so that lives will be touched by the fellowship I have found with the Holy Spirit. Lives will be heartened and transformed; the blind will see and the dead will rise to life, the wombs that are locked will be opened again by the touch of the Holy Spirit and the youth will be on fire for the Lord. Finally, and above all, the true word of God will be preached to all nations of the world, Amen.

Truth about the Holy Spirit

- A believer's heart is the Holy Spirit's home.
- Christ departed so that the Holy Spirit could be passed on and imparted into us.
- The Holy Spirit is God at work in our lives.
- When taught by the Holy Spirit we know the perfect will of God.
- Without the Holy Spirit a minister is helpless before a sinner needing a Saviour.
- He who has the Holy Spirit in his heart and the Scriptures in his hands has all he needs.

Beloved, we can never truly experience the Holy Spirit until we prepare a place for Him in our hearts. The Word of God gives many wonderful names to the Holy Spirit, but perhaps the most unadorned name is the most profound. He is often referred to in the Bible simply as "the Spirit".

This was the term that John the Baptist used when he described what occurred at the baptism of the Lord Jesus. He said, "I saw the Spirit descending from heaven like a dove, and it abode upon Him" (John 1:32). You might even call Him the unique Spirit, the one and only Spirit, for after all, in person, in work, and in our personal experience of His dwelling, there is none other like Him.

The Lord Jesus also used the same words. He declared to Nicodemus:

"Except a man be born of water and of the Spirit, he cannot enter into the kingdom of God" (John 3:5).

Again and again, we are encouraged to be "be filled with the Spirit (Ephesians 5:18; Acts 9:17). The names are given to the Holy Spirit that we may know about Him. They are names we can use every day in order to truly know Him and to welcome Him into the very closest aspects of our lives. Yes, He is the Spirit of the Father and the Son but He is ready to be our Paraclete, too, our Counsellor, our Helper, our Teacher, and our Guide. He is the Spirit of glory and grace, the Spirit of wisdom and knowledge and might. He is the very Spirit of the living God and of Jesus Christ in our lives today.

The Holy Spirit Brings about a Change

Beloved, one of the greatest things the Holy Spirit

does is to change our lives. He truly does. He changes people from the inside out—our lives, our circumstances, our perspectives. He wants to change you today as you read this book—if only you will allow Him. He will truly bring about a change in your life and your ministries, your marriage, your family, your home and your peace.

The work of the Holy Spirit can be found in all of the 66 books of the Bible. In the Book of Acts, He is sometimes referred to as "the Acts of the Apostles" and His work is referred to as "the Acts of the Holy Spirit". In the Book of Acts we see the dramatic changes that happened in the lives of the apostles and the hundred and twenty in the Upper Room because of their fellowship with the Holy Spirit. The same transformative process can happen to you if you allow Him into your life today. As you are reading this book, let us ask and pray that the Holy Spirit will enter you that you might experience such changes.

In the life of a believer The Holy Spirit is the catalyst for change that we share everywhere we go, nations will realign themselves and our churches will be transformed.

The Holy Spirit Helps Us Hear Deeper Truths

The Holy Spirit takes you beyond the realm of hearing with your ears and enables you to listen with your heart; He gives you understanding which comes from listening with your heart. This was what happened to me when I heard the voice of the Holy Spirit say to me: "Margaret, go and lay your hands on the dead man and command life back to him". That is the power of hearing through the Holy Spirit.

✻❧❦✻ The Holy Spirit Changes Your Speech

When the Holy Spirit comes into our lives, He will change our speech, as He did to those in the Upper Room— as they began to speak in other tongues, as the Spirit gave them utterances (Acts 2:4). When the Holy Spirit comes upon our lives He will change our behaviour. After the Holy Spirit came into the lives of Peter and John they were changed men. Instead of fearing the Jewish authorities they became bold and preached the gospel with much confidence (Acts 4:13).

Before I met with the Holy Spirit, my tongue was like the tongues of the devil, in those days I used to swear and my tongue was not used at all to bring glory to God. When the Holy Spirit entered into my life the mouth that used to be used to swear was transformed into a mouth of praise and worship, a mouth that could bring words of comfort to others. This is the transforming power of the Holy Spirit; allow Him today to change your tongue to become tongues of instructions, Amen.

95

The Holy Spirit Will Change Our Vision

The Holy Spirit can change your vision if you allow Him to. When we establish a fellowship with Him, He will change the things we see and how we see them. Instead of looking down in misery and depression He will cause us to see our lives and our world in a much brighter way.

Before my divine encounter with the Holy Spirit, I used to see myself as a failure and loser, unfulfilled in life and lacking hope or a future. But when the Holy Spirit came into my life my vision was turned away from self-pity and onto the glorious future—which is still unfolding. The Holy Spirit wants to change your vision today. He wants you to begin to see your future as bright and full of hope and love with the promise of paradise at its eventual end. Amen.

The Holy Spirit Brings about Change in Our Attitudes

The Holy Spirit can change our attitudes, beloved, if we welcome him into our hearts. Saul, who later became Paul, is a perfect example of the way He can transform our lives as He changed Saul's attitude and mindset— totally redirecting Saul's path and helping him find the purpose of his very existence.

The steps of the righteous are truly ordered by the

Lord. Praise God, God has divinely guided my footsteps and has turned me toward my true divine purpose. My attitude has changed for the better, thank God, and He is still working in my life to bring me to a mark of perfection. Amen.

The Holy Spirit is here to transform your attitudes if you are willing to let Him to lead you. Will you allow Him today, to change your attitudes and your outlook on life?

The Holy Spirit Will Change Our Prayer Lives

Beloved, it is impossible for any Christian to develop a prayer life without the help of the Holy Spirit. Once we know Him, our prayers will begin to follow naturally, yet apart from the Him, it is impossible. Beloved, before my encounter with the Holy Spirit I could never have prayed for five minutes and not run short of what to say. But when the Holy Spirit took over my life, sometimes, I am so lost in His presence that I don't know that time has gone for hours.

One glorious morning in 2004, I woke up with a desperate desire, a hunger, to worship the Lord and I started to pray in the Holy Ghost, speaking in tongues. Beloved, the Holy Spirit totally took over my prayer that morning and I spoke in tongues non-stop for eleven hours, unable to stop even when I tried. The Holy Spirit changed my prayer life from less than five minutes to over eleven hours in order to let me bask in His presence. All glory to the Lord. Amen.

When Peter was locked up in prison, the believers prayed for him unto God ceaselessly (Acts 12:5). The believers prayed unto God and He sent an angel to the prison to free Peter. He was set loose, the very chains binding his ankle falling away and releasing him (Acts 12:7). May the same power that came upon Peter in prison and set him loose visit you today as you read this book and deliver you in Jesus' name, Amen.

The Holy Spirit Will Make Your Calling Sure

The Holy Spirit will help to make our calling sure, beloved. Since the day the Holy Spirit called me to minister His word I have never looked back concerning my calling and assignment. In the past many people asked me how I was so sure of my calling, I simply replied that the Holy Spirit inside of me had spoken to me in words and visions, through dreams and through seasoned men and women of God.

In the Acts of Apostles there were those who were called by God for special assignment and the Holy Spirit said: "to separate Barnabas and Saul for the work where unto I have called them" (Acts 13:2). The church fasted, prayed laid hands on them and sent them on their way.

My special assignment is to heal the broken-hearted, to mend their wounds through the word of God. The Bible says; "So they were sent forth by the Holy Spirit to the Island of Cyprus" (Acts 13:4).

The Holy Spirit Is Our Teacher

Beloved, today you must ask the Holy Spirit to be your teacher. Begin now to talk to Him; He desires a fellowship with you. Take a decision today to spend time in contemplation with Him. He longs to be with you. Speak to Him in your prayers, and next time you open the Bible ask the Holy Spirit to show you what He wants to teach you. Ask Him to walk with you. Be sensitive to Him; please do not aggrieve my Holy Spirit.

As you begin to spend time with the Holy Spirit in your prayers He will become closer to us all: It is only prayer that will bring Him come close to you. When He moves, we should also move with Him, and He will help us when we minister and teach. He will give us sound counsel and advice. Often, when I don't know where to begin in my ministrations, the Holy Spirit will whisper in my ear: "Daughter be at peace, as you open your mouth I will fill it and teach you what to say". Amen.

The Day the Holy Spirit Came into My Life

Beloved, when I read Pastor Benny Hinn's book, Good Morning Holy Spirit and saw the level of hunger he had in his life for the Holy Spirit, I went on my knees and cried, saying: "Holy Spirit, please, I don't yet know you the way Pastor Benny is describing you, could you please make yourself real to me, Holy Spirit." That night, the Holy Spirit came fully into my life and my life has never been the same since. Thank you my precious, Holy Spirit.

Beloved, since I truly found the Holy Spirit, I have referred to Him as "My Precious Holy Spirit" for He truly is precious to me. He is closer than the air I breathe-in. He has become my guide and my lead, my advisor and my advocate, my comfort and my very best friend.

He is the one who whispers into my ear and shows me secret things. He is the one that speaks of events to come and brings them to pass. He is truly all I need and all I will ever need. I never want to grieve or sadden Him because He is so special to me.

When David prayed in Psalm 51 he said, "Please Lord, never take the Holy Spirit from me."

My, heart's cry is equal to this my Lord, "Please never take the Holy Spirit away from me. Amen". I hope that is your heart's cry as well. Amen. If you don't yet know the Holy Spirit intimately, this book is an opportunity for you to cleave to Him. He longs for fellowship with you, He wants to be your guide and He wants to be part of your life. Why not open your heart to Him today? I can assure you, you will never be disappointed that you did. The Bible says: "O Come, taste and see that the Lord is good" (Psalm 34:8). Amen.

How to Receive the Holy Spirit

If you would like to receive the infilling of the Holy Spirit, please use these Scriptures and I am sure, you will be truly filled in Jesus' name. Jesus said, how much more shall your heavenly Father give the Holy Spirit to those who ask Him? Father, fill your children with the Holy Spirit in the name of Jesus, Amen.

John 14:16-17:
"And I will pray the Father and He shall give you another 'Comforter' that He may abide with you forever. Even the Spirit of truth, whom the world cannot receive because it seeth Him not, neither knoweth him, but ye know him, for he dwelleth with you, and shall be in you".

Luke 11:3:
"If ye then, being evil, know how to give good gifts unto your children, how much more shall your heavenly Father give the Holy Spirit to them that ask him"?

Acts 1:8:

"But ye shall receive power, after that the Holy Ghost is come upon you, and ye shall be witnesses unto me both in Jerusalem, and in all Judaea, and in Samaria, and unto the uttermost part of the earth".

Acts 2:4:

"And they were all filled with the Holy Ghost, and began to speak with other tongues, as the Spirit gave them utterance".

Acts 10:45:

"And they of the circumcision, which believed were astonished, as many as came with Peter, because that on the Gentiles also was poured out the gift of the Holy Ghost".

Acts 19:5:

"When they heard this, they were baptized, in the name of the Lord".

Acts 19:6:

"And when Paul had laid his hands upon them, the Holy Ghost, came on them, and they spake with tongues and prophesied".

Romans 10:9:

"That if thou shall confess with thy mouth the Lord Jesus and shall believe in thine heart that God hath raised him from the dead, thou shall be saved".

Romans 10:10:

"For with the heart man believe unto righteousness, and with the mouth confession is made unto salvation".

Beloved, why not ask our precious Holy Spirit to fill your heart right now, open your mouth and begin to pray if you have been baptised in the Holy Ghost. Amen.

8

God's Warning for Shepherds

೧೩೮೦೧೩೮೦

God's Warning for Shepherds Not Feeding The Sheep and the Lamb.

Ezekiel 34:1-6

"And the word of the LORD came unto me, saying, Son of man, prophesy against the shepherds of Israel, prophesy, and say unto them, Thus saith the Lord GOD unto the shepherds; Woe be to the shepherds of Israel that do feed themselves! Should not the shepherds feed the flocks?

Ye eat the fat, and ye clothe you with the wool, ye kill them that are fed: but ye feed not the flock. The diseased have ye not strengthened, neither have ye healed that which was sick, neither have ye bound up that which was broken, neither have ye brought again that which was driven away, neither have ye sought that which was lost; but with force and with cruelty have ye ruled them.

And they were scattered, because there is no shepherd: and they became meat to all the beasts of the field, when they were scattered. My sheep wandered through all the mountains, and upon every high hill: yea, my flock was scattered upon all the face of the earth, and none did search or seek after them".

Beloved of the Lord, this particular chapter of the book was written out of my desperation and heartfelt pain for ministers of the gospel who knowingly or unknowingly abandoned their duties as shepherds of the Lord.

It was on the 5th of March in 2009, at about 12:20 a.m. when I heard the Spirit of the Lord say to me: "Margaret, my sheep are scattered about, my sheep are not fed, and they are malnourished. Those that are sick are not cared for, those that are broken—their wounds are not mended." The Lord said that those that are scattered have become a prey in the hands of the enemy.

The Lord said to me: "Go out there and tell my

Shepherds to repent and change their ways", or else He is going to bring judgement to them and that some of the shepherds are going to lose their lives. Some of the candlesticks will be removed. At first I thought Lord, this is going to be a hard job, I was not an expert in this subject and I thought that no one would take the word seriously enough.

I continued my prayer until early one morning, at about 3 a.m., I heard the Spirit of the Lord grieving in my room. I asked the Lord what the matter was and heard him say to me: "Margaret, why have you not blown the trumpet sound to alarm my shepherds who have not tended the sheep that God has given them? I broke down and wept, begging the Lord's mercy for my disobedience.

Beloved, why is the Lord angry with the shepherds?

The Lord is vexed because some shepherds have enriched themselves. They have gathered the choicest properties— the cars and the planes— yet the sheep under them are suffering. Some have turned their ministries into a market place, exploiting their anointing, while spending less time with the sheep.

Those that God has given us to nurture, how are we nurturing them? Those whom God has put under our various ministries to care and nurse them back to life, how are we caring for them? God is going to come beloved, suddenly, and remove some of these shepherds and their candlesticks will be removed and given to another. The Lord is sounding his warning now, at this hour; let those who have ears hear what the Spirit of the living God is saying to his failing churches.

In Ezekiel 34:7-10 the Word of God says:

"Therefore, you shepherds, hear the word of the Lord. As surely as I live, says the Sovereign Lord, you abandoned my flock and left them to be attacked by every wild animal. And though you are my shepherds, you didn't search for my sheep when they were lost. You took care of yourselves and left the sheep to starve".

Therefore, you shepherds, hear the word of the Lord. This is what the Sovereign Lord says:

"I now consider these shepherds my enemies, and I will hold them responsible for what has happen to my flock. I will take away their right to feed the flock, and I will stop them from feeding themselves. I will rescue my flock from their mouths; the sheep will no longer be their prey".

This passage of Scripture lays out the complaint of God against these poor shepherds of God's flock. They have failed in their duty and their charge before God and He rebukes them pointedly. In this passage of Scripture we can outline exactly what a shepherd of God's people is supposed to do and what he should be careful not to fall into.

We must understand that although the Lord is rebuking these pastors in terms of a shepherd and his flock, the analogy is exactly that of a spiritual leader of God's people and his relationship with his congregation. These sheep and lambs are at a point of spiritual death because of the neglect of their leaders.

"Shepherds that do feed themselves; should not the shepherds feed the flocks?"

Again, there is nothing wrong with a pastor who works of the gospel to live of the gospel—this is biblical and proper. But God is rebuking these particular shepherds because they lived well from the sheep, extremely well, in fact, and these men did not fulfil their part of doing a good job for a good salary. They took liberties with the goods and properties of their flocks and instead of reinvesting them into the needs and tasks they were supposed to they lived in luxury. Their primary objective— to feed, nurture and protect their flocks, they have failed dismally.

Feeding on the Word of God For Spiritual Growth and Reproduction

"Ye eat the fat, and ye clothe you with the wool, ye kill them that are fed: but ye feed not the flock".
— Ezekiel 34:3

Many shepherds, sadly, are not feeding themselves with the pure word of God any more. They are too busy running from one pole to the other, thereby neglecting the ministry of the Word. The apostles in the New Testament dedicated themselves to the ministry of the Word in order to be able to feed the sheep well. They were able to do this by appointing seven men that were filled with the Holy Spirit to help with the administration of the ministry. But here and now the Lord is concerned about the welfare of the sheep and the lambs.

The word of God, in Ezekiel 34 verse 4, says:

"The diseased have ye not strengthened, neither have ye healed that which was sick, neither have ye bound up that which was broken, neither have ye brought again that which was driven away, neither have ye sought that which was lost; but with force

110

and with cruelty have ye ruled them. Verse 5: "And they were scattered, because there is no shepherd: and they became meat to all the beasts of the field, when they were scattered".

Shepherds! God is sounding His trumpet to warn us that we must go out and bring back the lost sheep to the Lord. Right now, the doors of China and the Middle East are wide open, for truly the harvest is plentiful, who will go for Him?

This is the period when pastors and ministers should be sending out their evangelists and proselytisers to these nations, thereby, ministering the Word of the Lord to these lost souls in these nations. Our Muslim brothers and sisters need to hear the true Word of God, the Hindus and adherents to all the other false religions need to hear the gospel. ✂️🐚🐚✂️

What Are the Shepherds Doing at this Hour?

Some are too busy consolidating their own personal gains, forgetting the main reason why God called them into the ministry in the first place. May the anger of the Lord not be rekindled on any shepherds, let us take heed of His word now and mend our ways. The Lord is saying that He will take away the right to feed the sheep from these shepherds and will stop them from feeding on the sheep. This is very serious, beloved of the Lord, and sadly some God will have to remove because of the gross negligence in their duties as shepherds.

I once heard a story at a conference in Nigeria about a deliverance minister who took a young boy and said he needed to conduct deliverance for him. Unknown to the young boy, the minister took this boy and used him for ritual killing in order to increase his members in the church. This minister was meant to nurture, to set the captives free, but instead of nurturing this young boy he took him as prey. Lord, have mercy on these false shepherds, God will arise in His anger and destroy these wolves pretending to be ministers of the gospel. They have dragged the name of the Lord into mud. God said He will remove their candlesticks and some will be destroyed. Amen.

Where now is the fear of the Lord shepherds of the living God? Who has bewitched you?

In Galatians 3:1, Paul said:

"O you poor and silly and thoughtless and unreflecting and senseless Galatians! Who has fascinated or bewitched or cast a spell over you. Unto whom—right before your very eyes—Jesus Christ [the Messiah] was openly and graphically set forth and portrayed as crucified"?

Oh shepherds of the Lord, who has bewitched you, what has cast a spell over your mind? Who have blinded you that you are unable to see the truth anymore? The gods of this world have blinded your spiritual truth. Return to the Lord, because He will come quickly and will judge you and remove you from oppressing his sheep and lamb.

In the case of the deliverance minister who killed the young boy ritually in order to gain power and wealth something has clearly gone desperately wrong. Why are some ministers suddenly desperate to become wealthy? The giver of the assignment always provides whenever He calls us. Why are shepherds busy running from one end of the world to the other in order to chase material wealth? God is going to judge those shepherds, if they do not repent of their greed and take up their holy works.

Roles of Shepherds

The role of a shepherd is to serve and not to be served and Jesus was, and is still, the perfect example for us to follow. He humbled Himself by washing His servants' feet, which shows us that the best way to serve is by humbling ourselves, loving the sheep, nurturing them, teaching and admonishing them, mending their wounds and recovering the lost back to the Lord.

113

What Is Your Reward Going to Be, Shepherds?

Revelation 22:12:
"And, behold, I come quickly; and my reward is with me, to give every man according as his work shall be".

Beloved of the Lord, we all know that Jesus is returning soon, and that we expect to receive a reward or punishment according to how we have lived our lives here on Earth. God is the one who will diligently reward you according to how you spend your life here, but how do we intend to account to the Lord all that we have done? Have we examined our lives daily to see if we are living according to the word of the Lord and according to the paths and patterns He has given us? Are we keeping the commandments, the precepts?

God has already given each of us talents, gifts, and we are all going to be called to give account of how we have used them. Are we a good steward or bad one? Did we use all the talents, abilities and potential that God has charged us with to please Him?

Now, ministers of the Lord: that gift of healing that the Lord has given you, how are you using it? Have you been to the hospitals and to the halfway houses and the streets to lay-on hands and heal their sicknesses? That gift of deliverance that God has given you, have you exercised your power and authority over demons and subdued and banished them? You with the gift of prophesy, how are you using it? Are you giving the word that you receive from the Lord or are you selling it? Is your word glorifying God, Is it edifying the church of God?

Now you with the gift of faith, have you used it to lift people's faith in God for them to be able to receive from the Master? You, with the gifts of prosperity and wealth, are they used to build on the works of God or are you just collecting the money and buying planes and cars and vast estates for yourself? Are their widows and orphans, homeless people and those in the third world dying daily from lack of water, medicines, and housing as you increase your own wealth?

Is yours a gift of singing, of playing instruments in the house of God? These days, people are charging men and women of God fees to use their voices to praise their Creator. Is this how God intended it to be saints of the Living God? Are you now charging God for giving you these talents? You with gift of compassion, when was the last time you visited that elderly neighbour of yours? When last did you help that sister or brother who is depressed, when did you last go out of your way to raise and comfort someone who has given up hope? Did you know that just one word— one uplifting word could save someone from committing suicide?

The words that can save us today are these: On that fateful day when we will all stand before our Lord and Saviour to give account and to be rewarded, do you think the Lord will welcome you warmly as a faithful servant, rebuke you for wasting your talents or abjure you for failing Him completely? My prayer as you are reading this book is that we may all revisit our lives with sincerity and examine how we are living and know if we are pleasing the Lord, that no-one be cast out or abjured by Him.

"Blessed are they that do his commandments, that they may have right to the tree of life, and may enter in through the gates into the city" (Revelation 22:14).

9

Repairing the Broken Altar of God

Let Us Repair the Broken Altar of God in Our Churches and Our Lives.

Just as Elijah repaired the altar that had been broken, certain preparations must necessarily precede divine blessings. Repentance must be sought before divine intervention, you cannot continue to live in sin and expect God to bless you and your ministries, your businesses and homes. How can we continue to sin and expect the grace of God to abound in us?

How Have We Defiled the Altar of God?

Malachi 1:6-10:

"A son honoureth his father and a servant his Master; if then I be a Father, where is mine honour? And if I be a Master, where is my fear? Saith the Lord of Hosts unto you, O priests, that despise my name.

And ye say, wherein have we polluted thee? In that ye say, the table of the Lord is contemptible. And if ye offer the blind for sacrifice, is it not evil? And if ye offer the lame and sick, is it not evil?

Offer it now unto thy governor; will he be pleased with thee, or accept thy person? Saith the Lord of Hosts. And now, I pray you, beseech God that he will be gracious unto us: this hath been your means: will he regard your persons?

Saith the Lord of Hosts. Who is there even among you that would shut the doors for nought? Neither do ye kindle fire on mine altar for nought. I have no pleasure in you, saith the Lord of Hosts, neither will I accept an offering at your hand".

The Spirit of the Lord has ministered to me several times on the issue of broken altars, polluted and defiled altars and has placed a burden and a responsibility on ministers whose altars have been polluted.

Why Some of These Altars Have Become Polluted

Many minister's altars have become polluted

through the strange and selfish fires that have been allowed to spark and rekindle in their altars. Many ministers have allowed the love of money, power and political influence to overtake them. False ministers, who lie every day in their blasphemous use of the Lord's name, have buried human beings beneath their altars; on some day-old babies have been used in cruel, unchristian sacrifices.

Last year whilst on a visit to Nigeria, I had a vision of a well-known man of God. In this revelation the Lord showed me a grave on a piece of land, which I kicked at until, lo and behold, the gravestone was rolled away. I saw then what had been carved into the surface of the gravestone: "Here lies the body of this man of God".

The Lord told me that many ministers of God had laid the foundations of their churches and their ministries with sacrifices of an animal, the vulnerable or mentally ill, a pregnant woman or even a new-born baby upon their bloody altars. I was so shocked, almost disbelieving and the Spirit of the Lord told me that the man of God whom he had revealed to me had buried himself as the foundation of his church. That night I awoke my husband and told him what the Lord had revealed to me. He told me that not all which glitters is truly gold—that God had shown me what He had to— to expose some of these selfish and self-appointed arbiters of the Lord's will. May the Lord have mercy upon us, His faithful ministers, when so many of those who pretend to be amongst our numbers abandon their duties and poison their altars.

In another revelation that same night I had returned to sleep when the Lord opened my eyes with the vision of the Spirit and I saw in the sky the name of another supposed man of God. The Lord showed me the name of this man, which was written across the sky. Three times, I saw his name written and three times I saw a hand appear to wipe it away before and I heard the voice of the Lord once more, saying: "Do not look at it, it is heavily polluted. Do not look at the miracles".

I did not know who this man of God was. When I woke up I contacted a friend, a seasoned man of God who also lives in London and enquired as to whether he knew of any minister or similar by the name the Lord had shown me in the night. He answered immediately, telling me that the name belonged to a deliverance minister in Nigeria. I knew then that the message was indeed from God, beloved, and that so many ministers who started with hearts full of faith and earnest intentions had been corrupted because their focus had shifted from God our Lord to the venal gods of mammon.

It is God who has called us into the vineyard to work on His behalf, but many are not satisfied with the manner and moment in which the Lord has called them to their tasks; many are running and cutting corners, trying to stay ahead of their responsibilities to the divine purpose He has chosen for their lives.

Invited Guest Ministers

Another area in which the Lord ministered to me was in the area of inviting other ministers who are famous to speak in their various ministries. Many ministers make such choices with ill-chosen motives; they are not allowing themselves to be led by the Spirit of the Lord when inviting a guest minister to come and speak from behind their altars. Some of these ministers of God, sadly and though even they may not know it, are polluted. By bringing them to your churches and allowing them to minister at the altars of God you are thereby inviting spiritual corruption into your churches and allowing it to spread through your congregations.

God cannot honour our service and self-sacrifice when the altars are polluted, and our motives must be pure to keep our altars unspoiled. Are we inviting these men to raise money for our ministries or to draw larger crowds for us? Are we hoping to grow our congregations so that our own acclaim increases or so we might help set more people onto the paths that the Lord has laid out for them? Our motives, the spirits in which we undertake out Holy duties, are of grave importance to God. Let us invite only people in whom the Holy Spirit dwells richly and thrives for the service of God. Let us be careful and fear His displeasure and censure.

Stolen Money and Blood Money

Some ministers do not look too closely at the source of the money that is being brought to their altars in the name of thanksgiving. This is because they suspect, or know full well, that the persons who have brought the money are armed-robbers or corrupt politicians and bureaucrats who offer some of their stolen money to the altar of God, seeking to avoid punishment. Our God is not a thief and will not honour such offerings.

Blood money is ritual money: Some people have used human beings for rituals and bring this same money as offering to man or woman of God to bless. Some ministers do need to discern seriously before accepting monies because you do not know how they have come about these evil monies. Once the man of God accepts such blood money in your altar, the altar will become polluted and God will not accept that kind of sacrifices.

Malachi Chapter 1:14:
"But cursed be the deceiver which hath his flock a male, and vowed and sacrificeth unto the Lord a corrupt thing: for I am a great King, saith the Lord of

hosts, and my name is dreadful among the heathen".

The Word of God says that God will not do anything except He first reveals it to his servants the prophets. Today, the prophet of God is speaking to you concerning some of these polluted altars of God. The Lord is grieved about these and He wants you to change from your evil ways. Repent, if you want God to bless you and your ministries, your homes, your businesses and your marriages.

Joshua was marching to the Promised Land as miracles happened around him. First the wall of Jericho fell, but then he sent some soldiers against the small town of Ai and they were defeated. Joshua sought the face of the Lord concerning this, and revealed to him what had gone wrong. He was told to repair the altar that had been broken in

Joshua 7:10-13:
"And the Lord said unto Joshua, Get thee up, wherefore liest thou thus thy face? Israel hath sinned, and they have also transgressed my covenant which I commanded them: for they have even taken of the accursed thing, and have also stolen, and dissembled also, and they have put it even among their own stuff.

Therefore the children of Israel could not stand

before their enemies, but turned their backs before the enemies, because they were accursed: neither will I be with you any more, except ye destroy the accused from among you.

Up, sanctify the people, and say, Sanctify yourselves against to morrow: for thus saith the LORD God of Israel, There is an accursed thing in the midst of thee, O Israel: thou canst not stand before thine enemies, until ye take away the accursed thing from among you".

As you are reading this book the Lord wants to repair the altar of God that sits in your heart, my blessed and beloved. Decide, right now, that you are going to put everything right and rid yourself of anything that is not of God in the altar of your heart and in your ministries.

God desires to heal the broken altar of God in your life, check yourself thoroughly and make sure that there is no door left open, no altar that is broken and needs to be repaired. As Gideon had to destroy the altar of Baal, he replaced it with the new altar of God. What altar do you need to repair or build afresh today, my beloved of the Lord?

10
Prophetic Messages

The Word from the Lord after Ninety Days on the Mountain.

During the summer of 2011, I spent ninety days on the mountain in prayer and reflection in order to receive instruction from the Lord and learn of things that would come to pass in His name. Please read that which he told me carefully and with your spiritual mind ennobled by the Holy Spirit for the Bible says; let those who have ears hears what the Spirit of the living God is saying at this hour. Amen.

Prophecies and Messages Received by Margaret Ade Odusanya (Nee Mayaki)
Monday, 27 June 2011

America, City of Louisiana

"In Louisiana," said the Lord, "I am going to cause a revival and reawakening to happen shortly. This revival will lead to other states to follow. There is a well that has been opened up there, others will go and partake of it".

California City, California

"Because of the strange fire they have rekindled, I am going to set an earthquake there if they do not repent: the spirits of Sodom and Gomorra are in control of that land."

Kentucky

"Gather my people and pray for two days and nights in order that natural disasters not strike this state."

Louisville

"Pray against the great flood coming into this area. Hold four days of fasting, as a state, to avert this urgent peril. Amen".

Texas

"There will be a great change in governance in the State of Texas and there must be prayers to avert a collapse of law and order".

Washington, D.C.

"The Executive Branch of the government needs to pull together. A government divided cannot win the election and secure the future of a nation. Delay in this would cause a great loss of power during the next election and they need to seal the gap now".

Oklahoma

"In times past men and women of God have laboured in this part of America and God is going to bring a dividend there; sons and daughters are going to be raised and they will be blaze trails for God and His works. The seeds that were planted many years back are about to yield a bountiful harvest, Rejoice"!

The Middle East

"I am going to bring about a vast amount of changes in this region. I caused the convulsion of these lands to bring about the reawakening and the redemption of souls in this region. Truly the harvest is ripe now, this is the season to bring an evangelical fervour to the region so that those nations which have sat in darkness for too long, will begin again to see great light coming upon them. Wake-up and move in and possess the land," said the Lord, "The doors to these lands are open."

Nigeria—Innocents and Bloodshed

"In the land of Nigeria where the nation is not at war, yet they have shed far more innocent blood than necessary. The blood of the innocent is crying out across the land, but I am a God of Justice and I will avenge the innocent blood shed. The Boko Haram sect, that originally came from outside the nation entered through doors left open for many years but, there is a season for everything and power has to change hands now.

The nation's borders must be tightened. The intelligence services need to be reinforced so that they might kill the serpent now—before its offspring spreads and becomes too numerous to stop. This attack was targeted at the nation's stability and was meant to weaken the authority of the president who truly needs the spiritual guidance of the Lord and the true prophets of God.

Tell him not to look down on the servants of God whom I am sending to him, I am raising the unknown prophets whose hand has not been soiled for this season in Nigeria. Be sensitive in your spirit. Allow the perfect will of God to be done in the land. Accept that the Lord builds a house, that builders labour in vain and make God the centre of your administration that God might rebuild the nation again for you".

The Economy of the Nation

"Never allow those whose hearts are not in the building of the nation to come to positions of power. Allow the Lord to help you to discern and weigh those who offer counsel in prayer and alongside My anointed prophets" said the Spirit of the Lord. "It is well with you".

United Kingdom

National Women's Day of Prayer
"This event will usher a new fire into this land", said the Lord.

Doors of revival are going to be opened.

Women will take their places as watchmen.
Power will change hands.
Prophetic utterance will bring great change to the
realm of the Spirit.
Powers of witchcraft will be broken.
Sleeping churches will be reawakened.

Youths will begin to find their purposes and callings.
Major and a highly public death will occur, shaking
the nation.
Revivals will start to rekindle in cities.
Fear of God will take its place again across the land.
God will use the enemy of the gospel to cause a
change to the law that will affect Christians.

**The Word of the Lord from the Lord Concerning Things
to Come**

Prophesies Received by Margaret Ade Odusanya
(Nee Mayaki)
Thursday, 5 May 2011

Beloved, I had been on the mountain for over a
month waiting to receive from the Lord when he
gave me the following message that I might impart it

to His children. I speak not from my flesh but from my spirit, God bless you all. Amen.

In time past, I have shown you and told you that in 2011 a lot of Muslims will come to the knowledge of the Lord. We have seen the reawakening in the Middle East, which is going to open the door of Christianity to them and that many will come to the knowledge of the truth which is Me—Jesus Christ. Amen.

In the following years, there will be a lot of unrest coming from the Middle East, North Korea and China, with the death of Bin Laden marking the beginning of a great upheaval as his followers sprout up like grass to sow discord and mayhem.

Nations, particularly those in the West, will need to watch their borders especially closely and security round the President of the United States of America will need to maintain a constant vigil as attempts on his life will be made. Be full of prayers for him to avert the planned assaults from the pits of hell," said the Spirit of the living God.

My beloved, the seer sees deep in the spirit, sees what

others do not see, hears what others do not have the opportunity to hear and knows the heart and mind of Christ.

A seer or prophet has more grace to hear the heart of the Lord. In this hour God is raising powerful seers and prophets within the various nations of the world. The seal of God is going to rest more on them, their word will be sharper than any two-edged sword, and none of their words will fall to the ground. As I am revealing their fate to them, Ezekiel 12 will come to pass then, as they speak it, it is happening.

Today the world will see a great rise in the numbers of Deborahs and mothers in Israel. I will begin to shrieve the true prophets of God in this season," saith the Spirit of the living God. Those who seek to bring my name down into the mud shall be exposed and removed.

A lot of candlesticks are going to be put off as they are of no more use to me. The candlesticks in some churches are dead and can no more bring light to the church. I am the light of the world. I am the fire from which others come to light their candles".

Prophesies Received by Margaret Ade Odusanya (Nee

Mayaki)
Wednesday, 7 July 2010

To the Nation of Nigeria

The Lord said that there is a major disaster coming to Nigeria and that he would send me to bring them a warning. The Lord said, that they need to turn from their wickedness, that their cup is almost full:

Tell them that I, the Lord, the mighty Jehovah, have sent you to them. Tell them that the rod of my judgement is set ready to strike their nation if they do not turn and repent. The churches think they are praying. What they are doing is like a child's play. I am the God of justice and I will judge them. But there is still a chance now if only they will harken to the voice of their God and repent and turn away from their wickedness. The nation that does not fear God, that nation is preparing for doom. Tell them that this is their time to change, this is their moment to begin again to diligently seek My face, for if they seek My face while am near, they will find Me.

What Must Nigeria Quickly Do to Avoid Disaster?

133

Repent from sins and wickedness.

Cleanse the land from all evil—idols, fetishes, etc. and purge out all unholy things.

Use the blood of Jesus to wash themselves and their land.

Begin to care for the less privileged.

Leadership will need to be replaced with godly men and women.

House of Jacob and the church of God Zion needs to rise up and take their places.

Hold three days of national fasting and prayer, with prayers of consecration and cleansing made over the land as soon as possible.

Do not toy or tarry with this message. The Lord said to learn from the mistake made by America and the disaster in the Gulf of Mexico— which swamped them in the crude oil they were so greedy for.

For the Nation of Nicaragua

The Lord is about to root out ungodly men who are trying to oppose His work in that nation. "Only the remnants will remain there, for there is going to be purging in those lands," saith the Lord, "Tell them that there is going to be tumult and upheaval. Only the fervent prayers of the saints will enable the work of God there to be firmly planted. Tell the church to rise up from their sleep, that the Lord said they have been too long where they are and that the church of God seems to have been sleeping".

Papa Billy Graham

The Lord said that Papa Billy is soon to come home, that his time here is very short. The Lord said that he has fought the good fight of faith and that his crown and his place in heaven are already prepared for him.

UK: National Women's Day of Prayer

The Lord spoke to me again and told me that after this day of prayer has been undertaken, "The light of God will begin again to shine forth in this land. Slowly but surely My Word will again be established. The churches must unite together. Together they will accomplish more. No single tree can make a forest but together, they will be stronger and they will achieve their purpose and My plan for the land".

Messages Received by Margaret Ade Odusanya (Nee

Mayaki)
Thursday, 30 October 2010

Beloved of the Lord, today the Lord gave me this message for the nations of the world. Please read it and key into what God is saying at this time in Jesus' name. Amen.

My people are destroyed for lack of knowledge (Hosea.4: 6). Kings are set in place to take instructions from prophets. To receive knowledge, they must seek the counsel of wise prophets. The tide has changed now when seasoned prophets will be sought again for instructions on the way forward.

This morning, daughter, I am again sounding my trumpets to nations to harken unto my voice and my will. Nations that humble themselves before me in these perilous times will find peace and abundance in their lands.

The United Kingdom and other Nations

This is a period of famine in the lands of the UK and several other nations. Where are the Josephs of the land? Where are the Nehemiahs of the land? Where are the Shadrachs, Meschaks, and the Abednegos of

the land in this season? I seek a man that will stand
and pray to turn the tide of woes that has befallen
these nations.

Behold, I am God, the God of all flesh. Is there
anything I cannot accomplish in these present times
my children? For if they truly will repent from their
sins and their wickedness and turn away and cry out
to me then I will hear from heaven and heal their
lands again.

Nothing will happen except I first reveal it to my
prophets, if they will not look unto the vessel and if
they will truly harken to the Holy Spirit, then peace
will reign in their time.

God's Children Around the World

Hear the sound of abundance, of rain being poured
on my faithful ones. I have set before them tables of
riches, blessings, salvation and deliverance. My well
is deep and the source of it is pure. Come and drink
freely and you will thirst no more.

As the year is drawing to a close, let my children
diligently seek me and know the will and the heart of
God. The enemy is yet again preparing to drain and

feed off the life-blood of the innocent, but when they come before me I will steer their vessels to safety that no evil might befall them.

South Pacific

"Pray against major disasters in the South Pacific area, my people there need to fast and pray in earnest to avert a terrible earthquakes and tsunami".

Silicon Valley

"In the Silicon Valley of California a bud is being grown that will cause financial mayhem and cause a loss of income in the billions. Let the people in that area pray and be alert to this danger".

An Urgent Message from the Lord for the United States of America

Messages Received by Margaret Ade Odusanya (Nee Mayaki)
Thursday, 31 January 2010

Saints of God, the Lord gave me a message for the United States of America, but for the past two weeks I have struggled with it. I love America. I have friends and relatives there and am totally committed to the well being of their nation, but I fear the import of this message might be lost. Nonetheless it is time to release this message to the world so that we can all pray and ask God's intervention, that the perfect will of the Lord might be done.

The Lord said that the nation of America: needs to repent, that she needs to go down on her knees crying and weeping and to beg his mercy. America is meddling in the affairs of Israel, the place where His blood was shed and also the place of His birth. The Lord said that any country that will not support Israel totally will be dealt with, and that America needs to quickly repent so that judgement will not come upon the land. "The nation of America was once great but is now only a shadow of itself", saith the Lord. "Tell my people who are called by my name to begin three days of prayers, to be said all across the land, and crying aloud to the Lord for forgiveness that their land might be healed and restored".

The Lord wants all intercessors to stand in the gap for America and wail before the Lord. I see a storm coming to America in a scale unheard of and never before seen, and only with fervent prayers will this be averted. Pray, America, pray.

I am a jealous God, and I do not share my glory with anyone. America has turned her back on the only true and wise God and has gone after the gods of this world of mammon, who have blinded them and left them unable to see the punishment at the end of the road they follow. For restoration to come to America, commit three days for national prayers, fasting and crying out your repentance. Do not meddle in the affairs of Israel again, only tell the truth and stand solidly behind them and pray for the nation of Israel, because this is my homeland and my heartbeat.

The Lord said to pick seven men of God to go to the White House and pray for the president, that seven is the order of perfection. The seven men must be men that have no blood on their hands, no deceits in their hearts nor the love of money. Pray for the perfect will of the Lord for the president, pray against sudden death and attack from the quarters he least expects. A prayer of consecration must be made over him to anoint him for the office. Pray and lay hands on the president.

The Lord said unto me: "Do not take this message

lightly, for these are my commands to America. Once this is done, I the Lord will once again hear their prayers and heal their lands."

As the prophet of God, I have to deliver this message and pray that all of us who have the best interests of America at heart will pray and stand in the breach for her. I am only a mouthpiece of God in this and am sworn to obey His perfect will.

God Bless America!

Author's contact:

megodusanya@yahoo.co.uk
www.brokenheartedministries.com

Lightning Source UK Ltd.
Milton Keynes UK
UKOW032337220213

206705UK00007B/150/P